Writing Excellence

Lee Clark Johns

ADAPTED BY LEO SEVIGNY

THOMSON

DELMAR LEARNING   Australia Canada Mexico Singapore Spain United Kingdom United States

Writing Excellence
Lee Clark Johns

Vice President, Career Education Strategic Business Unit:
Dawn Gerrain

Director of Editorial:
Sherry Gomoll

Acquisitions Editor:
Martine Edwards

Developmental Editor:
Gerald O'Malley

Editorial Assistant:
Jennifer Anderson

Director of Production:
Wendy A. Troeger

Production Manager:
J. P. Henkel

Production Editor:
Nina Tucciarelli

Director of Marketing:
Wendy E. Mapstone

Channel Manager:
Gerard McAvey

Library of Congress Cataloging-in-Publication Data

Johns, Lee Clark.
    Writing excellence / Lee Clark Johns ; adapted by Leo Sevigny.
        p. cm.
    Includes bibliographical references and index.
    ISBN-13: 978-1-4018-8203-7 (alk. paper)
1. English language—Rhetoric—Handbooks, manuals, etc. 2. Technical writing—Handbooks, manuals, etc. 3. Business writing—Handbooks, manuals, etc. 4. Report writing—Handbooks, manuals, etc. I. Sevigny, Leo. II. Title.
PE1408.J67 2005
808'.0666—dc22   2005009900

NOTICE TO THE READER

To everyone who "writes for a living"—
which means almost all working adults.

Contents at a Glance

Contents

>>

< vii >

Chapter 4   Writing   65

Chapter 5   Editing   89

Chapter 6   Refining   124

Writing Excellence is a practical manual. It walks you through the writing process—from planning, organizing, and writing strategies applied to both long and short documents, to editing and revising final drafts. Its flexible writing models work in different professions, companies, and organizations. This manual replaces the traditional "how-to" texts for different business writing genres (reports, memos, letters), with a commonsense decision-making process that taps your critical thinking skills and experience.

As a workplace writer, or student preparing to enter the workplace, you have the content knowledge and talent. But other members of your team—coworkers, customers, management, vendors, regulators, and the public—need to understand what you know. To ensure you meet their needs, you will profit from coaching that helps you

> ➤ Move from adequate writing to excellent.
> ➤ Ensure that your ideas are clear.
> ➤ Prevent misunderstandings and problems.
> ➤ Save time in your writing.
> ➤ Increase your confidence about your written products.

The goal here is to help you develop strategies, visualize successful options, practice the plays, and learn the rules of effective workplace writing.

LEE CLARK JOHNS, the owner of Strategic Communication, Inc., a consulting and training company, has been teaching business and technical writing for 25 years. She has worked with everyone from corporate executives, to bankers, to attorneys, to customer service representatives. From them, she has learned that plain English is preferred over the more ornate, literary style of writing taught in college. *Writing Excellence* reflects what she has learned from her clients and students.

Introduction

>>

Whether you are searching for your ideal job or are satisfied with the position you have, today's rapidly changing workplace requires constant personal and professional development. Savvy employees and job seekers understand the need to be prepared for inevitable changes in corporate structure, new job opportunities, and personal lifestyle. The *Pathway to Excellence* series is for anyone looking to build a foundation of effective communication skills, job search techniques, and a personal success plan for growth and promotion in any industry.

The series delivers real-life skills and strategies that can be applied immediately to your personal or professional life. This book provides a comprehensive guide for success when read cover to cover. The straightforward approach of the text also makes it an excellent reference if you have limited time and need specific advice by topic.

Icons used throughout the book help to highlight key points and exercises.

 Exercises for you to complete

 A helpful perspective on how to accomplish the goal at hand

 A list of common mistakes to be on the lookout for

 A summary of the main points of each chapter

However you make use of the insights in this series, our hope is that you continue to pursue your individual *Path to Excellence*.

Introduction to the Writing Process

Your Goal: Reader-Friendly Documents

For too long, business and technical writing has focused on the wrong person—the writer, not the reader. Instead of concentrating on what will make the reader's job easier, professional writing often has emphasized the writer—what language and organization are easiest for him or her.

This manual presents strategies to help you make your writing reader-friendly. This term does *not* mean that your ideas are simple or uncomplicated. Often, in professional settings, the ideas to be conveyed are quite complex. But the documents explaining them need not be. To aid, rather than inhibit, your reader's grasp of your ideas, you must have:

> I assume that readers are burdened, harassed, and furiously distracted. . . . My strongest wish is not to waste their time or impose on them.
>
> SAUL BELLOW

> ➤ A clear understanding of your audience and purpose for writing.
> ➤ A logical organizational plan with a main idea up front to guide your reader.
> ➤ A good balance of clearly stated key points and supporting evidence.
> ➤ Words that are appropriate and clear to your reader.
> ➤ Sentences that are clear and grammatically correct.

These elements shape the Writing Process, a model for writing clear, complete, and correct documents. This manual follows this process, with each

< 1 >

chapter addressing the elements in more detail. Each begins with an overview, followed by explanations, exercises, and samples. Used with permission of the writers and their companies, all samples are actual workplace documents representing the kinds of writing people do each day—reporting results, making proposals, transmitting information, solving problems, giving instructions, and corresponding with associates inside and outside their organizations.

The manual's goal is to help you, too, become a reader-friendly writer.

The Writing Process

To use your writing time efficiently, think of writing as a process, not a product. Most of us rarely produce a first-time-perfect document. Instead, we go through a series of steps that lead to the final product. People's writing processes differ, and individuals vary their practice depending on the type of document. You will save time and produce clearer documents if you concentrate on one step at a time as shown in Table 1-1.

YOUR TURN

Self-Assessment Activity

Purpose: Analyze your own writing practices. If you are creating a significant document (not a brief note or routine form), what percentage of your writing time do you spend:

Prewriting _____

Writing _____

Rewriting _____

TABLE 1-1.	The Writing Process	
Stage	Step	What to Do
Prewriting	**Planning**	• Analyze your audience(s). • Identify your purpose (or reason for writing). • Brainstorm to generate ideas.
	Organizing	• Prepare a blueprint (or outline). • Put your main idea up front. • Arrange key points in order. • Identify action wanted.
Writing	**Drafting**	• Write a draft. • Emphasize key points. • Focus each paragraph. • Impose a clear order.
Rewriting	**Editing**	• Evaluate clarity and precision of words. • Eliminate unnecessary words. • Tighten sentences.
	Refining	• Correct errors in grammar, punctuation, mechanics, and spelling. • Format text.

TIPS

The Case for Managing the Writing Process

Many people cut short one or more steps in the writing process. They feel there is not ample time to plan and proofread, or they are too quick to finish.

The problem is that short-cutting a stage in the writing process often wastes time. Without a good map or blueprint to direct your writing, ideas wander. Such drafts either bury the main idea and key points where the reader won't find them, or they require extensive (and inefficient) reconstruction during the rewriting stage. If you skimp on proofreading, you risk looking careless with your written product and perhaps your other work products. ■

People often say, "I don't have time to plan." But if you want to become a reader-friendly writer, you don't have time NOT to plan.

Professional writers say the art of writing is rewriting—where you achieve the fine polish of great writing. But most workplace writers do not need to spend that much time polishing. There is a point at which you need to send the document. However, really important documents may require a high degree of revision. More important, all documents deserve significant planning and organizing before the writing begins. This planning will help you to achieve consistency and an effective voice in your writing.

Planning

Potential Problems	Strategies
Document does not focus on readers' needs	Analyze all your potential readers: > What do they know? > What do they need to know? > What vocabulary are they familiar with?
Readers wonder, "Why am I reading this?"	Ask yourself, "Why am I writing?" Then tell your readers up front. Think about how and when your readers will use the document. Plan a format that makes the information easily accessible.
Most prominent ideas are stale, or important ideas are buried.	Use brainstorming techniques to discover your best ideas—*before* you write.

< 5 >

Planning

Planning

< 6 >

Planning the Document

Planning is the foundation of your writing. Earlier I lamented the fact that much business writing is written for the writers, not the potential readers. To succeed, you need to plan your document to meet your readers' needs as well as to achieve your purpose.

During prewriting, you face five basic decisions that help shape your writing strategy. These decisions lay the foundation for choosing content, shaping an organizational blueprint, determining an appropriate style, and even designing the document's format. The decisions are:

> Who are my audiences?
> What is my purpose?
> What is my main idea?

> What are my key points?
> What is the action I want?

PITFALLS

The Temptation of "Binge Writing"

Many times in the workplace, you must write a memo or important e-mail under the gun. Time is short, the pressure is on, and all eyes are on you. Resist the temptation to fire off that memo without planning, organizing, and rewriting. You may think there's no time for the process, but looking organized and professional are worth the effort.

Remember that spelling and grammar checkers are not fail-safe; the computer software is not to blame for your errors. So write your document and pause. Take a minute or two away to increase your objectivity as you review. Better yet, ask someone else to read it and give you some quick feedback. ■

Planning Decisions

The planning decisions discussed in this chapter are critically important because they determine content, style, and format. Unfortunately, writers often jump directly to "What do I want to say?" (content) without first answering these foundational questions—"to whom?" and "why?"—that analyze the context in which they are writing.

Decision One—Who are my audiences?

> Who will read what I am writing?
> How many different readers are there, and are their needs the same?
> What do the readers expect from my document?
> What information do they need?
> What information do they not need?
> What technical language do we share?
> How receptive are the readers to my message? Hostile? Sympathetic? Neutral?
> Who will do what I want done? Make the decision? Solve the problem?

Decision Two—What is my purpose?

> Why am I writing?
> Is it primarily an informational or a persuasive document?
> How will readers use the document?
> Do different sections have different purposes?
> How should I state why I am writing?

> I don't want to know how the watch was made. I just want to know what to do with it.
>
> –A COMPANY PRESIDENT

Decision One: Who Are Your Audiences?

First, answer this central question: "Who will read this document?" It is difficult to write reader-friendly documents without an answer. You can use several techniques to analyze your readers.

Approach One: Analyzing Reader Interest

This approach looks at what information your readers want to know and what vocabulary they share with you.

	These Readers Want to Know:	In What Style?
Lay Readers —anyone outside your field	The big picture; general issues and details; "What's in it for me?" (WIIFM). They do not want technical detail.	Plain English

	These Readers Want to Know:	In What Style?

Management
—anyone who
  has oversight
  responsibilities
	The big picture, with particular focus on financial issues: What's it going to cost and what will be the return on investment? They want to know, "What's in it for the company?" (WIIFC).	Plain English

Experts
—your
  professional
  peers
	All the technical details. They may need your document to do their own work. They also will be checking to see whether they agree with your analysis.	Technical language (jargon) is clear, precise, and concise for these readers.

Technicians
—people who will
  do the hands-on
  work
	Some of the technical details, particularly those related to "how to" and "why." They do not want to know everything you know.	Plain English and some jargon.

Approach Two: Analyzing Audience Importance

This method analyzes how different readers will use your document and which readers are most important to target.

Readers	What They Will Do with Your Document
Primary	The reader(s) who will do what you want done: make the decision, solve the problem, follow the procedure, answer your question. If you have to choose whose needs to meet, you should choose the primary reader(s).
Secondary	The readers who will receive your document for information only. At some point, they may use your document, but right now you are only keeping them informed.

Don't make false assumptions:

- That your readers will read the entire document. Many won't.
- That the addressee and the primary audience are the same. Often, the addressee is your pipeline to the primary reader.

Intermediary The readers who will review your document before it reaches your primary reader(s). They may include your supervisor, an administrative assistant, a manager, your client contacts who will pass the document on to their decision makers. These readers/reviewers have real power over your document, but they are not the decision makers.

Approach Three: Analyzing Your Audience's Expertise

A third way to analyze the complexity of your audiences is to think about who shares your expertise. You will have readers who share some of your knowledge about your organization, the project, and your profession—but not all of it.

A key to your success is understanding how complex your potential audience is. Many people attempt to communicate and have important information to share with management, team members, or clients, but they miss the mark by not tailoring their writing to match the needs of those readers.

Understanding Your Audience

This exercise will help you to determine who your target audience is. Answer the following questions by listing either the names or categories of your own readers.

Who normally reads what I write? (Who is the audience that I write to?) _____

Who else might see what I write, both internal and external readers? (Who are the other possible readers?) _____

Although unlikely, if something goes wrong, who else might read what I write? (Whose hands might my document fall into?) _____

> Remember: The question is not "To whom do I write?" The question is "Who might read what I write?"

Workplace Application— Audience Analysis

The audience-unfriendly memo shown in Figure 2-1 was actually sent to people working for this manager. How do you think the readers will react? What results do you think the manager wants? Will the memo achieve those results? If not, why? What would you change?

Date: May 1, 200___
To: Department Personnel
From: Manager
Subject: Vacation and Work Break Policies

I have noticed in recent weeks a lack of understanding regarding this department's vacation policy. To clarify this matter, I strongly suggest the following guidelines be adhered to:

1) Vacations should be taken only when absolutely necessary. Do not take a week's vacation simply to get away from the company. (If you need to be away from the company that badly, you are probably ready for a change of jobs.)

2) Vacations should be scheduled so as to cause the least negative effect to the company. Plan your work well in advance and leave no loose ends when you do go on vacation.

3) Although the company has granted you two weeks' vacation, do not feel compelled to use the entire two weeks. Unexpected emergencies such as illness or a death in your immediate family, could well put you in a negative position for next year's vacation.

4) Before deciding to use your vacation, you should request counseling time with me. In many cases, sensible discussion will help avoid unpleasant situations later on.

If you have any questions on any of these guidelines, I will be more than happy to discuss them with you. Due to the length of this memo, work break policies will be addressed in a subsequent memo.

Figure 2-1: Audience-Unfriendly Memo

Decision Two: What Is Your Purpose?

Why Am I Writing?

Writers often confuse their business purpose (or the problem to be solved) with their writing purpose. The business purpose is the issue they are addressing; the writing purpose is why they are writing the document. Readers usually want to know what you *learned,* not what you *did.*

In planning, you should think about both the business purpose and the writing purpose. Both will usually appear in your first paragraph, and the writing purpose often states the main idea.

Two very general purposes—to inform and to persuade—cover all documents. However, analyzing your purpose more specifically will help you focus the document. For example, a procedure is obviously written to inform. But you will write a better procedure if you identify its purpose as to teach or instruct.

Exercise: List five more specific reasons (purposes) for writing documents:

1._____

2._____

3._____

4._____

5._____

Workplace Application—Analyzing Audience and Purpose

For the following product evaluation in Figure 2-2, analyze the writer's sensitivity to his audience and purpose. As you read this first page of a four-page software evaluation, think about how he meets his readers' needs. Who do you think his readers are? What is his writing purpose? What else might he do to make this long document reader-friendly?

Author: I.S. Analyst   **Composed:** 07/11 11:41 AM

Subject: Computer Master Management as a Development Tool

Overview

Computer Master Management is marketed as an end-user relational database management system and reporting tool, but it has features that (many people believe) place it nearly in competition with professional Client/Server development tools such as ProPower. This paper will examine Management as a development environment and attempt to identify the situations where its use is appropriate (and where not).

What Makes Management So Attractive?

Management was designed as an end-user tool. It is far more easily mastered than any of the current crop of "professional application" development tools. Raw development productivity, especially at first, is easily an order of magnitude faster with Management than with a professional tool such as ProPower.

Figure 2-2: Analyzing audience and purpose

Planning

Other features are:

- Being a Computer Master product with a huge installed base of users, Management is far more stable than most development tools.
- Management's script language is Visual Basic, which is an easy-to-learn language that many people already know.
- User interface windows can be rapidly created by simply specifying a database table, and the windows are strung together to build applications through the use of "Macros." Many applications can be built without writing any code.
- The report writer is extremely powerful and easy to use—it makes the report writers that are bundled with most development tools look primitive in comparison.
- Connections are provided to enterprise-level databases such as Supercompute, which allow these databases to be manipulated in the same ways that local Management databases are manipulated. This makes it possible to use Management as a development tool for enterprise databases.

So Why Not Use Management for Everything?

Management has the potential to someday be grown by Computer Master into a professional development tool that would compete directly with ProPower. But right now, Management is not yet an industrial-strength application development tool:

- Management source code is stored in a Management database, rather than ASCII files. Version control options are extremely limited and entirely Management-specific. One such third-party product is known to exist: "Management Monitor."
- Team development is very difficult, for the same reason. Externally, a Management program looks like a single, monolithic DBS file. Although you can place that file on a LAN server and share it, all the developers have write access and can easily destroy each other's work.

[The report continued for three more pages and ended with . . .]

Summary

Management is an extremely powerful and valuable tool for end-users and a few classes of professionally developed applications. It is not an appropriate choice for the types of industrial-quality applications that I.S. is usually concerned with building.

I.S. should develop the expertise to support the product and should encourage (and manage) its use among the user community. Some means must be found to manage the expectations that Management generates.

Your Analysis

> Who do you think his readers are?
> What does he do to meet his readers' needs?
> What is his writing purpose?
> What else might he do to make this long document reader-friendly?

Purposes for Writing

Persuasive

Your purpose is persuasive if you want your readers to do something: approve your proposal, buy your product, agree with you, or follow your instructions. Most workplace writing involves some form of persuasion.

Informative

Your purpose is informative if you are simply conveying information that readers need.

Persuasive	Informative
Analyze	Announce
Criticize	Answer
Demand	Ask
Deny	Confirm
Discuss	Congratulate
Entertain	Document
Explain	Inform
Instruct/Teach	Invite
Justify	Thank
Praise	Transmit
Propose	Update
Recommend	
Report	Others?
Request	
Sell	
Suggest	

Others?

YOUR TURN

Revising to Clarify Purpose

Purpose: Revise the memo to John Legal in Figure 2-3 by focusing clearly on its purpose. Why is the writer sending this second request? (The first memo must not have been clear either.) Based on the purpose you identify, rewrite it to state that purpose and clarify the content for the reader.

```
INTEROFFICE CORRESPONDENCE

Date:     November 27, 200__
To:       John Legal
From:     Alice Accounting
Subject:  APEX LABORATORIES (Second Request)

The work performed on the above contract was started before the contract was
executed; thus it is required that the authority to do this be appropriately docu-
mented. Please send this to my attention so that I can attach it to the contract.

This contract is over $50,000, and because of the changes made on this standard
form, a preexecution review by the Legal Department should have been completed
and documented on or with the contract. Because this contract is for $100,000,
insurance verification is required.

If you have any questions, my extension is 5436.

cc: Contract File
```

Figure 2-3: Revising to clarify purpose

Brainstorming to Generate Ideas

What Might I Want to Say?

Many people start writing to discover what they want to say. That freewriting
technique is useful if you need to discover a topic, but most workplace writers
already know what they need to write about. With freewriting, you risk getting locked into an organizational structure too early in the writing process.
As a result, obvious ideas are up front, your fresh ideas and key points are
buried, and revision requires a lot of frustrating reconstruction time.

You can avoid these problems by using brainstorming techniques to generate ideas. Instead of writing full sentences and paragraphs, use these mind-
opening strategies to discover your best ideas—*before* you write.

When brainstorming, use phrases in a laundry list if you are a word person, or draw a diagram if you are a picture person. Use any medium to brainstorm: scratch paper, butcher paper, the computer, Post-its on a wall. The point is to generate a free flow of ideas before you begin to decide which ones to include in the focused, logically ordered blueprint of your document.

Using Words

For proposals	List Pros and Cons for what you are proposing.
For justifications or explanations	Jot down the Point and Reasons.
For informational documents	List the 5 Ws and H: Who, What, When, Where, Why, and How.
For problem-solving documents	Identify . . . • the Problem • the Solution • the Action you want the reader to take
For procedures	List The Actor The Act

ELEMENTS OF EXCELLENCE

Chapter 2 focused on how you can effectively plan your writing. In this chapter the following points were explained:

> You discovered questions that you can ask yourself to effectively plan your writing.

> You learned how understanding your audience helps to focus your writing.

> You learned the importance of targeting a particular purpose.

> You gained brainstorming techniques you can use to develop your ideas.

Organizing

Potential Problems	Strategies
Document is a story of what the writer did, with the main idea and key points buried.	Outline your main idea, key points, and support using the ideas and details generated during brainstorming.
Conclusions and recommendations are buried.	Distill the most important points to put in an Overview up front.
Reader gets lost because the document lacks logical order or the order is not apparent.	Use formatting techniques (headings, white space) to highlight your logical progression.

Chapter 3

>>>>>>>

Organizing

Organizing

< 18 >

Organizing

Organizing the Document

If your goal is to create documents that are reader-friendly, information must be logically arranged and packaged for easy access by readers. In a sense, good organization creates a map for your readers by telling them the main idea of the document (your information destination), the major key points along the way, and the response you need from them when they reach the destination. Like a well-drawn map, a well-organized document is predictable.

You focus your readers' expectations by:

> Including an Overview at the beginning of longer documents.
> Using point-first structures: main idea in the first paragraph and key points at the beginning of body paragraphs.
> Using content-oriented headings throughout the document.
> Breaking up heavy text with white space, headings, columns, and **bold** key terms.
> Substituting graphics and meaningful captions for text, when appropriate.

During planning, you identified your audiences and targeted your purpose. This chapter covers the organizing decisions that complete the Prewriting Stage:

Decision Three—What is my main idea?
If I could write only one sentence to make my point, what would I say?

Decision Four—What are my key points?
If I could explain briefly, in only a few sentences, what would I say?

Decision Five—What is the action I want?
What do I want the reader(s) to do?

The answers to these questions form the map that guides your readers through all documents—from very long reports, to proposals, to shorter memoranda, letters, and e-mail. The central question is, "How can I organize information to make the reader's job as easy as possible?"

The Process: Drawing the Map

From your brainstormed ideas generated during planning, you are now ready to make decisions about content and order.

First, review your material.

> Identify your key points by grouping related items and giving them a label.

> Drop items that are not relevant to this audience and purpose, even though they may be true.

> Look for content gaps. Have you overlooked any significant details? Do you need to gather more information to support some points?

Second, based on your audience analysis, arrange your key points in descending order of importance to your primary audience(s). In workplace writing, this order often moves from quantifiable issues (e.g., cost, productivity) to softer issues (e.g., image, morale).

Finally, write a working main idea. Although you write it last, it will appear in the first paragraph of your document to guide your readers. In a sense, the main idea is a contract you make with your readers, promising to give them certain information in a certain order.

Organizing Shorter Documents

You should have an overall map or blueprint for organizing your ideas in shorter documents. The diagram in Figure 3-1 helps you visualize how the parts of a one- to two-page document fit together. It also turns the brainstorming from Planning into a clearly organized document blueprint.

Decision Three: What Is My Main Idea?

Your main idea is the point you are trying to make. It is the answer to the question, "If I could write only one sentence and it couldn't be long, what would I say?"

In a short memo, letter, or e-mail, one sentence should clearly and concisely state your most important message. If your document does not take a position (as in a request for information or answers to several questions), the statement of purpose replaces a main idea.

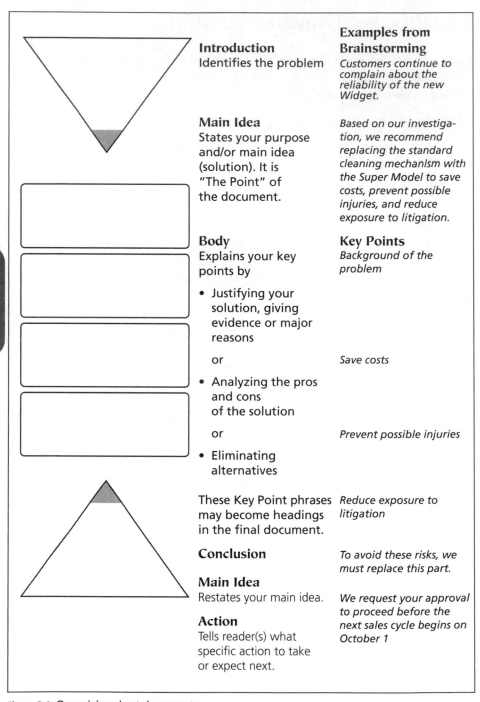

Introduction
Identifies the problem

Examples from Brainstorming
Customers continue to complain about the reliability of the new Widget.

Main Idea
States your purpose and/or main idea (solution). It is "The Point" of the document.

Based on our investigation, we recommend replacing the standard cleaning mechanism with the Super Model to save costs, prevent possible injuries, and reduce exposure to litigation.

Body
Explains your key points by

Key Points
Background of the problem

• Justifying your solution, giving evidence or major reasons

or

Save costs

• Analyzing the pros and cons of the solution

or

Prevent possible injuries

• Eliminating alternatives

These Key Point phrases may become headings in the final document.

Reduce exposure to litigation

Conclusion

To avoid these risks, we must replace this part.

Main Idea
Restates your main idea.

We request your approval to proceed before the next sales cycle begins on October 1

Action
Tells reader(s) what specific action to take or expect next.

Figure 3-1: Organizing short documents

The main idea *should* state your judgment on the subject you are addressing. Sometimes it also briefly summarizes the key points to follow:

Despite the initial cost, we recommend purchasing the XYZ equipment to reduce ongoing operational and maintenance costs and to improve departmental efficiency.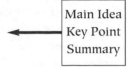

The main idea *should not:*

> Be incomplete. It must be a sentence that clearly conveys the point of your document.
> Be a question. Do not force your readers to guess your main idea.
> Contain hedgers such as "I think." If you make the statement, you obviously think it.
> Be vague or garbled. For example, "This issue has some significant ramifications for the economic situation of the corporation" does not say anything. Get to the point. Be clear: "To prevent further loss of market share, we must increase our sales efforts immediately."

Your subject line has high priority.
The subject line is critical in attracting readers' attention, especially in e-mail. A good subject line contains your reduced main idea, not just the general topic you are addressing. It also permits efficient retrieval if readers need to find your document in a file. Therefore,

Instead of
Subject: Brochure Copy

Write
Subject: Approval of Brochure Copy Needed by Oct. 1

PITFALLS

You have probably experienced situations in which you began reading a document only to find yourself wondering what the point was. Avoid letting your writing drift among ideas and details by putting your main idea up front.

Having a clear main idea is important both for you and for your readers. In the organizing stage, writing a working main idea helps you clarify and control your ideas. In the final document, the refined main idea tells your readers where you are headed. ■

Decision Four: What Are My Key Points?

Each paragraph in your document should make a key point that helps advance your main idea. In organizing your overall document, you identify the key points and arrange them in logical order. Your readers expect to find the key point at the beginning of each body paragraph, followed by details or further explanation.

Workplace Application—Analyzing a Good Memo

The entertaining memo about conference room space was widely read and remembered for several reasons. Think about what you like about it; identify the main idea, key points, and action.

From: Susan Smiley
To: All Employees
Subject: Use of Conference Room Space
Date: Wednesday, June 21, 200_, 10:28 a.m.

We continue to have a problem with what one might term "conference room terrorists," i.e., people who have a tendency to engage in the following search and destroy tactics:

- Assume they can commandeer conference room space without checking to see if the space has already been reserved;

- Don't adhere to the schedule and don't evacuate the room when time is up (this is why there are so many nose prints on the glass windows . . .);

- Book space, decide on a different mission, and then disappear into the jungle without canceling the space;

- Use a conference room for two or three commandos when an office or workstation would serve the same purpose;

- Seize the space reserved by someone else without proper advance warning.

I'm attempting a somewhat humorous (that remains to be seen, I guess) approach to an enemy which has plagued us for years—lack of conference space. You would think that with 15 conference rooms, we could find a place to gather the troops peacefully.

Analyzing a good memo

There are always extenuating circumstances which force all of us to be flexible from time to time—special meetings which arise suddenly, unexpected visitors, lots of people decided that they just HAD to go to YOUR meeting, and you didn't plan enough space—the list goes on and on. HOWEVER, practice basic courtesy with your fellow employees; I would hate to have to go out on a search-and-rescue mission after you don't . . . I prefer to use words as my weapon of choice.

Use the conference room scheduler. It's a great device—even I know how to use it, believe it or not. If I can, just about anyone who knows how to turn on the PC can. It's possible that we can make some refinements to this system to help you even more. It's a secret operation—don't call Linda or Jane; they don't know yet, either. We'll keep you posted.

Along other lines, all conference rooms will no longer be available for use by any employee or outsider for any profit-making purpose, regardless of whether such meeting might be at noon or after hours and even if these rooms aren't being used by anyone else for business reasons. Conference rooms can be reserved to host group meetings for professional organizations of which employees are members, and they will continue to be available for any employee-related function, such as birthday celebrations, wedding/baby showers, going-away parties, etc. Use the regular conference room scheduler for these events. The only codicil: if the room is required for a business purpose, that takes precedence over any non-business reason, but use the same guidelines discussed above!

If you have any questions as to whether or not your particular purpose meets the criteria, please contact the HR Department. We'll be wearing our regulation flak jackets.

Workplace Application—Reorganizing for Clarity

The e-mail that follows was sent to managers to enlist their help in orienting their new employees; it was routinely ignored. The original e-mail content focused on giving *information* about the Human Resource (HR) Department's program and what HR needed from the manager. In the revised version, the writer saw his purpose as *persuasive:* Here is what HR needs to help the manager and the bank successfully orient the new employee and reduce employee turnover.

In analyzing the original, answer these questions:

> What is the main idea and where do you find it?
> What are the key points?
> What is the manager supposed to do?

Starting recently, the Human Resource Department has implemented a new all day (8:30–4:30) orientation process to assist in reducing the bank's turnover. Included in the new program is the involvement of managers and regional managers. We will be serving lunch between 11:30 a.m. through 12:30 p.m. and would like all managers, available to attend, to join their new employee for lunch in the Bank Café. **(If you are available to attend please meet in the Human Resources office at 11:25; also, please remember to wear your name tags.) Please notify me of your availability as soon as possible.**

To ensure accuracy on all new hires, please complete the following forms for new employees:

- Survey of Applicant Quality
- Supervisor Checklist

Upon completion, please route to the attention of H.R. Jones at mail stop 1.3. For all supervisors' convenience I also enclosed a "New Hire Information" Worksheet. This provides management with the resources needed for obtaining system access. If any additional information is needed or if you have a scheduling problem for lunch, please contact me at my extension listed below.

Please remember to obtain the computer System Request Form, schedule the appropriate training and companywide orientation.

Thank you,

H. R. Jones

City Bank, N.A.
Human Resource Assistant
(566) 555-5555

Original e-mail

Notice how the order of key points and the format change in the revised version that follows.

> What is the main idea and where do you find it?
> What are the key points?
> What is the manager supposed to do? Notice how easy the action will be.

The Human Resource Department has implemented a new, all-day (8:30–4:30) orientation process to assist in reducing the bank's turnover. If you are a manager involved with completing paperwork and orientating new employee(s), your participation is needed in several ways:

- **Free food!** Who can pass this up?! To involve the managers, we are providing lunch in the Bank Café on orientation day. You are encouraged to attend with your new employee(s) and meet in the Human Resources office at 11:25 a.m. If you plan to attend, please RSVP by the Thursday prior to orientation. *(Please remember to wear your name tags for those of us who are forgetful!)*

- **To ensure accuracy on all new hires, please complete the following for new employees:**

  1. Please submit a **"System Request Form"** on all new employees to set up their user profiles. The attached link will direct you to Data Security's home page. Select the appropriate System Request Form for your department, fill in the appropriate information and click "Submit."

     (http://www.exchange.com)
     For your convenience I have also attached a **"New Hire Information"** worksheet (the attached file name is: employee's last name, first name_id.doc). This gives you the resources you need to complete the System Request Form properly and thoroughly.

     <<Sampson, Susan_M022221.doc>>

  2. Supervisor Checklist
     <<Supervisor checklist.doc>> *Due Friday following orientation*

  3. Survey of Applicant Quality
     <<Applicant Quality Survey.doc>> *Due Friday following orientation*

Please send the Supervisor Checklist and the Survey of Applicant Quality to H. R. Jones at mail stop 1.3 or e-mail to hrjones@bank.com.

If I can help or if you have a scheduling problem for lunch, please call me at my extension listed below. Your support is greatly appreciated.

H. R. Jones

Human Resources Representative
City Bank N. A.
566-555-5555

Revised e-mail

Reorganizing a Memorandum

Purpose: The following memorandum lacks clear focus. It covers most (not all) of the relevant information, but focuses on what the contest is, not on what might appeal to art instructors. The memo is not wrong; it just will not generate much enthusiasm. Your assignment is to transform it from "adequate" to "excellent."

Develop a blueprint for a new memo that is more persuasive. First think about the specific purpose of the memo. Then, what would art instructors want to know and what would motivate them to have students participate in the contest? Who else might read the memo? Brainstorm possible content. Then, create a blueprint for the memo using traditional outline form, the diagram model for short documents, clusters, or a flow chart. Do *not* rewrite the original memo. The point is to practice organizing before you write full sentences and paragraphs.

MEMORANDUM

TO: Art Instructors
FROM: Executive Director
SUBJECT: Youth Art Contest
DATE: April 17, 200_

Enclosed is information about a youth art contest Outdoor Boys and Girls is sponsoring in connection with our spring fund-raiser, JUST PLANE FUN.

We're looking for entries from boys and girls in Kindergarten through 12th grade. As indicated, the theme is aviation—to correspond to the theme of our fund-raiser.

All entries will be displayed at the event on Saturday, June 3, at the Aviation Jet Center at Brookside Airport. Winners will be selected by popular vote from the attending guests.

JUST PLANE FUN generates income that helps pay program fees for boys and girls whose families might not be able to afford participation in Outdoor programs. The contest offers a way for adults attending the fund-raiser to connect with youth.

Don't hesitate to contact us if you have any questions or need more information.

Reorganizing a memorandum

Decision Five: What Is the Action I Want?

Readers are often frustrated by documents that make them wade through explanation to find the answer to "What am I supposed to do?" The easy response form in Figure 3-2 meets readers' needs by:

> ➤ Putting the request for action up front.
> ➤ Making the readers' choices clear with a visual layout.
> ➤ Delaying the background to the end as an explanatory footnote.

These days, effective workplace writers are building in their response form at the end of a standard memo or letter. If the document is easy to return or fax, writers are more likely to get a quick response. E-mail programs also permit an immediate response, so building your action item into the text allows your readers to respond promptly.

Organizing Longer Documents

Long documents, those of more than two pages, can be particularly challenging to write for several reasons.

> ➤ They are long and, therefore, require time for the writer and the reader.
> ➤ They are usually not written at one sitting, so it is easy for the writer to lose focus.
> ➤ They are often the result of a team project with multiple authors and reviewers, who have different opinions about content and different styles.
> ➤ Readers probably will not read them all at one time. In fact, many readers will read only part of the document, not the whole.
> ➤ They can be very important, carrying high stakes and a long shelf life.

Long documents require an organizational strategy that allows you to efficiently manage both the writing and the document review process. Your strategy should also produce a document that gives readers a clear map up front and allows easy access to the information they need.

PAYER'S REQUEST FOR TAXPAYER IDENTIFICATION NUMBER

Please complete this questionnaire (all 3 items) and return it in the enclosed envelope as soon as possible.

1. Nature of your business with Pipe Line Company (CHECK ONLY ONE):

    [ ] Provide *services* (even though some goods may be provided)
    [ ] Provide *goods* (even though some services may be provided)
    [ ] *Rent* property, equipment or right-of-way
    [ ] Provide *medical* or health care services
    [ ] Provide *legal* services
    [ ] Received payment for *damages*
    [ ] Other (explain) _____

2. Please CHECK ONLY ONE in either A or B:

    A. Generally exempt from information reporting because my company is:

    [ ] Corporation   [ ] Pipe Line Company
    [ ] Tax Exempt Organization [ ] Governmental Agency

    ———————————————————OR———————————————————

    B. Not exempt from information reporting because I am:

    [ ] Individual or Sole Proprietorship
    [ ] Partnership

3. Taxpayer Identification Number (TIN):
   (COMPLETE ONLY ONE BOX BELOW)

   Taxpayer Identification Number

   _ _ - _ _ _ _ _ _ _

     OR

   Social Security Number

   _ _ _ - _ _ - _ _ _ _

Signature _____ Date _____

NOTE: The U.S. Internal Revenue Code requires us to report payments we have made for services. We are required to include the Payee's TIN on Form 1099. You are required by law to provide us with your correct Taxpayer Identification Number. If you do not provide us with your correct number, you may be subject to civil or criminal penalties imposed by law. The Tax Compliance Act of 1983 requires us to withhold 20% of payment reportable on Form 1099 unless the Payee's correct TIN has been furnished.

Figure 3-2: Making action easy

Figure 3-3 presents a reader-friendly model for longer documents. Not only is it useful for all types of technical documents, but it also works well for organizing feasibility studies, product evaluations, engineering plans, long proposals, audit reports, workforce analyses—in other words, any complex document with multiple sections.

TIPS

Our orientation is different when we are reading versus writing. Understanding this difference will help you to better manage your writing process.

> ➤ Writers work from bottom to top. First they collect all the data that is documented in the Appendix. Then they choose the most important information to analyze in the Discussion. Finally, they write the Overview, which contains the conclusions and recommendations—the big picture.
> ➤ Readers work from top to bottom, with the size of the audience decreasing as the report becomes more detailed.
> ➤ Different sections of the Discussion may have different audiences and purposes, as outlined in the report format that follows.   ▪

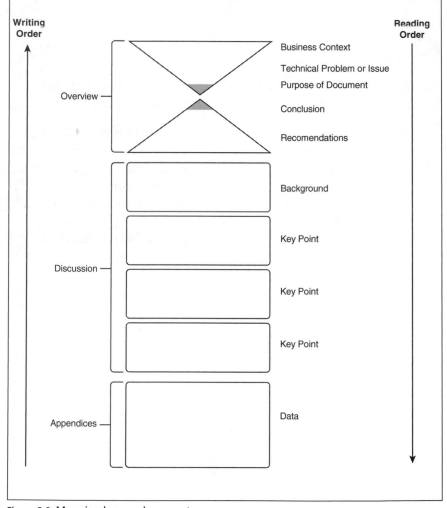

Model for Mapping Longer Documents

Writing Order
We write from bottom to top: Collect all the data, choose the most important to discuss, and then reach conclusions and recommendations.

Reading Order
We read from top to bottom: Readers want to know the big picture in an Overview before they encounter the explanation and details in the Discussion.

Writing Order

Reading Order

Overview

Business Context
Technical Problem or Issue
Purpose of Document
Conclusion
Recomendations

Discussion

Background

Key Point

Key Point

Key Point

Appendices

Data

Figure 3-3: Mapping longer documents

Organizing

Model Report Format

This format is set up in four components: Preliminaries, Overview, Discussion, and Appendix. These distinct sections are designed for different purposes and audiences. Some parts are always needed; others are optional, depending on the content. In this model format, the optional sections are **[bracketed]**. The goal is to provide a useful but *flexible* model for writing longer reports (over two pages).

Preliminaries Component

Audience/Purpose: The readers of the transmittal letter, abstract, and other preliminaries include all potential readers of the report, including anyone who may be searching for information in published or on-line indices. Therefore, the preliminaries should allow searchers to make an informed decision about the significance of the work and their interest in reading the entire document.

[Transmittal Letter]	A one-page letter that presents the major business or technical reasons for writing the report and what the report accomplished.
[Abstract]	A brief statement of the purpose of the technical work and significant findings (no more than 250 words). The abstract should not merely list the content of the report or the nature of the technical work. Instead, it should present the big picture.
[Title Page]	**Title of Report** Should inform the reader about the business benefit as well as the technical subject.

      Not: A Report on XYZ Modeling
      But: Modeling XYZ to Increase Oil
             Recovery in ABC

      Author(s)
      Date

[Table of Contents]	For reports over five pages.
[Lists of Figures and Tables]	

Organizing

Overview Component

Audience/Purpose: The Overview allows general readers (management or lay readers) to grasp the significance of the technical work: The reason it was undertaken, important findings and recommendations, and the benefits to the company and to their groups.

Style: The Overview should be written for a lay audience. Headings should be informative. Use lists of items when appropriate, because white space improves readability.

Business Context	Identifies the business reason for doing this study—the benefits to the organization—and then briefly describes the technical problem you attempted to solve or analyze.
Purpose	Briefly states the purpose of the report.
[Objectives]	What specific objectives or questions did the study address?
[Methodology]	Briefly outlines the experimental method, *only* if the method itself is critical to understanding the conclusions and recommendations.
Conclusions	Lists the major results and/or conclusions. These can be further developed in the Discussion component.
Recommendations	Lists recommendations for action or next steps by management and/or operations.
Cost Statement	This section *briefly* outlines the cost of the recommended action(s).

Discussion Component

Audience/Purpose: The Discussion (or body) of the report develops the ideas presented in the Overview. Written primarily for other technical experts and for informed readers, it allows you to fully explain technical objectives, methodology, findings, and the logic leading to conclusions and recommendations. The Discussion transfers the important technical information to readers who will improve operations. Therefore, it should focus on significant points rather than reporting all data.

To quote one manager, the Overview "should be written in language that anyone, including managers, can understand."

Style/Format: Although clarity is still a goal, using technical language (jargon) is appropriate in the Discussion. Adding informative headings and subheadings will help readers grasp the content of each section and will permit easy reference. Clearly focused tables and graphs may be included, but detailed graphics and calculations belong in the Appendix.

The nature of the technical work and the intended audience(s) and purpose should dictate the content of the report and the order for arranging sections. Workplace audiences generally expect to see sections arranged in *decreasing* order of importance or from general to specific. The following list includes possibilities, *not* requirements, for sections in the Discussion.

Possible Sections	Content
Problem Statement	What technical problem did the study address?
Specific Technical Questions or Tasks	What were the technical objectives? These may be posed as questions.
Background of the Problem	What was the history leading up to the current study?
[Pertinent Assumptions]	What assumptions limit the applicability of the study?
[Study Background]	What research has been done before?
[Definitions]	What special terms need to be defined so that all readers understand?
Technical Procedure	The description of the procedure should include only information that is necessary to understanding the findings, conclusions, and recommendations. Detailed documentation of the method should appear in the Appendix.
Results or Findings	What were the results of the technical work? How did the findings answer the technical questions posed?
[Cost Analysis]	If the report recommendations require funding, a thorough analysis of current versus future costs is important.
[Schedule]	If a new project will result from the study, identify the chronology of tasks, perhaps in a timeline.

Possible Sections	Content
Conclusions	What conclusions have been drawn from the findings? This section elaborates on the list of conclusions in the Overview component.
Recommendations	What actions should be taken based on the conclusions? This section also elaborates on the list of recommendations in the Overview.
[Future Work]	What future work is needed to complete the investigation or what additional questions has the study raised?
[Bibliography/ References]	What sources did you consult during the study? What references would the reader(s) need to know about?

Appendix Component

Audience/Purpose: The Appendix documents the entire technical effort. It includes the data and very detailed information of interest primarily to other experts.

Content: The Appendix may include:

> Theory
> Mathematical development
> Equipment
> Experimental or testing procedure
> Literature or patent search
> Data and results
> Site study
> Workpapers
> Detailed graphs, tables, charts, drawings, photographs

Workplace Application—Internal Audit Report

The report in Figure 3-4 applies this report format to a standard workplace document—an internal audit report. Mandated by an innovative manager, the format challenged the traditional audit report formats widely used by internal audit departments. Instead of placing Scope and Objectives (what the auditors looked at during their investigation) and background up front, this report meets the needs of the *primary audiences:* the manager and key

Report Overview Component

Confidential—Internal Audit Report

Company	Petroleum, Inc.	**Audit Subject and Location**	Petroleum, Inc.—Supply and Distribution and Wholesale Marketing
Audit No.			
Audit Date	August 24, 200_		Local City, State

Summary Audit Results:

Our audit of the Petroleum, Inc., Supply and Distribution (S&D) and Whole-sale Marketing Departments indicated excellent compliance by both departments to internal and operational controls in the areas of exchange and spot contract administration and documentation, supply forecast and inventory control information systems, and wholesale product pricing. Our review, however, indicated the need for Management attention to: ◄── Conclusion

• Using database software to operate current department information systems more effectively,

• Implementing a refined products quality control program,   ◄── Recommendations

• Expanding retail sales forecast procedures, and

• Establishing freight verification procedures.

Mr. _____ and Ms. _____ agreed to the audit comments and recommendations. Mr. _____ indicated that the implementation of improvements relative   ◄── Action
to quality control, sales forecasting and freight verification procedures would depend on involvement by the Retail Division and the Accounting Department. Presently, the S&D Department has been assigned neither the specific responsibility nor the staff to direct such activities.

Please read and reply as indicated using the response format set out on the reverse side. Forward your reply and other comments to:	GENERAL AUDITOR

Copies or Excerpts to:	Location:	Paragraphs	Reply Required	
CEO	Central, State	All	No	
President	Central, State	All	No	▶ Actions
Division Manager	Local City, State	All	No	
Group Manager	Local City, State	All	Yes ◄── Primary Reader
Audit Manager	Central, State	All	No	
Big Eight Auditor	Central, State	All	No	
Central Files	Central, State	All	No	

Your Copy	Approved by:	Audit Manager	Date:	August 26, 200_

Figure 3-4: Internal audit report

Organizing (vertical text)

Report Discussion Component

TO: Audit Manager   DATE: August 26, 200_

FROM: Auditors

SUBJECT: Petroleum, Inc.   Reference: PE000-00
             Supply and Distribution
             and Wholesale Marketing of
             Finished Product

I.   Audit Summary
Introduction

An internal audit of the Supply and Distribution and Wholesale
Marketing Departments of Petroleum, Inc. was performed during the
period of June 9 through July 25, 200_. The audit was completed by
Tom Smith and Julia Johnson and included three weeks of fieldwork
at the Local City Refinery.

The audit scope and objectives are summarized in Section II of this
report.

Audit Issues: Control Practices and Procedures

The results of our audit indicated excellent compliance by the two
departments, Supply and Distribution and Wholesale Marketing, in   ◄——   **Main Conclusion**
carrying out their functions in accordance with Management's
directives.

During the first quarter of 200_, the efforts of both departments were
plagued significantly by ESI software problems affecting the truck
rack reporting system, unfavorable variances in exchange, wholesale,
and retail demand, volatile market prices, and the performance of a   ◄——   **Problems Being Addressed**
refinery turnaround. Continuing attention, however, appears to be
directed toward each of these areas as well as toward developing
integrated strategies of inventory control and marketing.

Audit issues requiring Management's consideration and action noted
during the audit were as follows:

Figure 3-4: Internal audit report

To: Audit Manager
Prepared by: Auditors
Date: August 26, 200_

A. The Supply and Distribution Department should evaluate the feasibility of networking department microcomputers using database software to operate current department information systems more effectively. ←── Recommendation

During our audit, we reviewed the Supply and Distribution (S&D) Department's various information systems relating to forecasting, inventory control, and product scheduling. We noted several instances in which the same information is used repeatedly and input to different microcomputers.

Presently, these S&D systems are not integrated, and an information database does not exist. Consequently, all communication of information between staff members must be done manually. The data used at each microcomputer workstation must be input separately into each spreadsheet or report used by that system. ←── Problem Identified

In the absence of an integrated system, the potential exists for the following:

- Input error
- Inconsistent information
- Inefficient time usage ←── Potential Effects
- Inadequate response time needed to analyze changes in production or the marketplace

Consolidation of data across the functional areas of forecasting, inventory control, and scheduling should improve the quality of information in addition to streamlining information gathering procedures. ←── Benefits of Change

Discussion with Management

Since the audit, Group Manager has initiated discussions with a consultant currently contracted to establish database systems for the Transportation Department. Manager has also emphasized input quality control procedures to improve information generated by the present systems. ←── Actions Taken

[The report presented the three additional findings, which have been omitted here. They followed the same structure.]

Figure 3-4: Internal audit report

Organizing

Subject: Supply, Distribution & Marketing
of Finished Product
Audit
Ref: PE000-00

To: Audit Manager
Prepared by: Auditors
Date: August 26, 200_

Page 4

II. Audit Scope and Objectives

Our audit scope encompassed supply, distribution, and marketing activities during the twelve months preceding the audit, with particular emphasis on January through May 200_. Also included was a limited review of Petroleum's International spot market transactions.

← Documentation for Other Auditors

The primary objectives of the audit were to assess the reasonableness of:

- Supply forecast and inventory control information systems,
- Exchange and spot contract administration and documentation,
- Wholesale product pricing and marketing procedures, and
- Exchange accounting procedures.

III. Audit Conclusion

A draft copy of the report was reviewed by Manager and Director. General concurrence to the audit recommendations was expressed. To complete the audit process on a timely basis, a written response is requested from Manager by September 26, 200__.

← Action

We wish to express our appreciation to the staff members in both the Supply and Distribution and the Wholesale Marketing Departments as well as in International for the excellent cooperation and assistance we received during our audit.

← Courtesies

_____
Internal Audit Manager

_____
Senior Auditor

_____
Associate Auditor

Figure 3-4: Internal audit report

Organizing

individuals who will use the report's recommendations to improve operations. They want to know:

> ➤ How are we doing?
> ➤ What do we need to change to do better?

Those two questions are answered in the Overview page, and the recommendation comes first in each finding (note: Only one finding out of four has been included). The documentation of the Scope and Objectives (of interest to other auditors as secondary readers) is held until the end of the report, with the courtesies. This report achieves its primary purpose—to recommend four ways to improve operations in the Supply and Distribution and the Wholesale Marketing departments of Petroleum, Inc.—by putting the recommendations up front where management expects them.

YOUR TURN

Writing an Overview

Purpose: The next article appeared in the September issue of a public school system's newsletter to taxpayers and system employees. It explains how the superintendent and the school district are handling continuing budget cuts that threaten to hurt the quality of public school instruction. You will find the major points buried deep in the article, probably reflecting the superintendent's assumption that people will read the entire article (a faulty assumption). With this indirect plan, he risks annoying his audience. A more straightforward approach—overview with big picture up front—would give busy readers the information they want and probably ensure that more people would read the entire article.

For this exercise, based on the superintendent's audience and purpose, go through the process of developing an Overview.

1. Highlight the information that you think should be up front in an Overview. Look for *ideas*, not full sentences.

2. Construct a general map (or outline) for the Overview.

3. Write an Overview for the article that would summarize the major points citizens and employees would want to know.

If you want more practice, use the same article content to prepare an Overview for a report to the school board on the current budget crisis. Would you choose the same information? Would you organize it in the same order? Would the style and format be the same?

Superintendent Explains Difficulty in Setting Year's Operating Budget

Dear Patrons and Employees:

I would like to take this opportunity to extend greetings to you from the office of the superintendent for the first time for this school year. I feel that the new school year offers every indication of being a very excellent one for those most directly involved with the schools, the students and the staff members, and should also provide many satisfying moments for parents as they place the responsibility in the hands of the professional staff members for the education of their youngsters.

As has been communicated through the media during the summer months, it was necessary that I make some difficult recommendations to the school board, and for the school board to make some difficult decisions as part of the budgeting process for the school year. Although inflation is proceeding at a rate greater than 13 percent so far during this calendar year, the increases in expenditures for staff, materials and the overall programs within the school system amount to slightly more than 8 percent. This 8 percent increase in expenditures was built into the school year budget, a budget which provides for only a 4.5 percent increase in revenue for the next school year. Obviously, with the revenue falling almost 4 percent below expenditures and almost 8 percent below inflationary cost increases, it will not be possible for this school system next year and, in all likelihood, in years to come, to maintain the same levels of programming and staffing within the school system.

For the most part the more than 150 cuts in this year's budget were made in the noninstructional areas, such as a 37 percent reduction in the custodial force, a 13 percent reduction in the maintenance force, and other total elimination of departments such as the Staff Development Department and the Graphic Arts Department. Further reductions in administrative and administrative-related support personnel have now reduced expenditures in administrative costs within the school system to approximately $750,000.

As we begin our budget planning for next year and the years ahead, it is very obvious that further reductions in expenditures are going to be required. I am very concerned with some of the reductions in instructional program areas which were required to be made for this next year, such as a 50 percent reduction in the number of teacher aides in the schools, the reduction of staff in the Diagnostic Instruction Program and the various other program reductions which had to be made. These are just a preview of more extensive cuts to come in instructional program areas for the years ahead.

Writing an overview

As a result of the enrollment decline, I do feel that some further consolidation of staff, programs, and facilities within the school system can be accomplished as we've been doing in the past number of years. However, we cannot continue to make many further reductions in the years ahead without, in my opinion, seriously impairing the instructional programs in the schools.

In addition to spending a considerable portion of my time and effort in the months ahead attempting to identify further areas in which expenditures can be reduced in the school system, I will also be seeking ways of increasing revenue for this school system. City Public Schools simply cannot continue to offer the high level of programming which has been offered in the past many years with such a tremendous gap between inflationary cost increases and revenue increases provided for this school system. Recently you have been hearing of some "victories" for the taxpayers in our county. I would urge that each time you read of such victories, that you first of all pause for a moment and consider whether these victories might not in fact be a defeat for our children in the schools. All of us are concerned about taxes, but, at the same time, all of us should also be concerned about maintaining the same high level of instructional programs in this school system in which we have taken such great pride in the past. To not do so would be a real disservice to our children and to the community as a whole.

The challenges facing this school system—and this entire community—are very real and difficult. But citizens, given the opportunity, have always responded to the educational needs of their children. I feel confident that the combined efforts of citizens who place a high priority on the education of children and the dedicated, professional staff of this school system will result in the ultimate resolution of our common problems.

Best wishes for a successful school year.

John Smith

Superintendent

Organizing Your Brainstormed Ideas

The following pages illustrate how to organize your ideas. These models are useful for organizing all types of documents—proposals, memoranda, letters, e-mail messages, and procedures.

> Pros and Cons	For proposals or the benefit/risk section of a longer document.
> Point and Reasons	For justifications or explanations of why you are suggesting an idea.
> 5 Ws and H	For purely informational documents such as minutes, trip reports, or meeting announcements.
> Problem/Solution/Action	For problem-solving documents of all types. This is a common pattern in all business documents, including the overview of a longer document.
> Actor/Act	For procedures.

In longer documents, you may use different methods to organize different sections. For example, you would identify pros and cons to brainstorm the benefits versus risks section and the 5 Ws and H for a detailed project schedule.

Organizing a Proposal

There are many right ways to organize a proposal. As in all documents, content and organization are determined by who will read your proposal, who will make the decision, and what is most important to those readers. However, certain guidelines help you plan.

> If the proposal is lengthy (more than two pages), follow the report format principles that package information in different sections.
> Always include a brief management summary in plain English up front that includes what you are proposing, benefits (pros) to the "buyer," and the action you are requesting.
> Always include the cost, preferably early in the proposal. That's the information your readers are looking for.
> Based on your brainstormed pros and cons, make concessions or address risks to establish your credibility. If possible, offset each concession with a pro.
> Remember to include WIIFM or WIIFC—What's in it for me (the reader) or what's in it for the company.

Many proposal formats exist. Some are even mandated by organizations. If that's the case with your organization or intended audience, follow those guidelines carefully. If you have more flexibility, adapt the following format to match your readers' expectations.

Overview

The Overview, sometimes called an *executive summary,* contains the most important information for the most readers. It gives the big picture. It will be the only part of the proposal many people read. The overview includes:

Request	What is being proposed?
Business Context	What is the business issue being addressed?
Benefits	How will the proposed solution help the organization (the pros)?
Key Questions	What specific issues are you addressing?
Conclusions	What answers did your investigation reveal?
Recommendations	What actions do you recommend?
Investment	What will it cost and what will be the return on investment?

Discussion

The Discussion explains your reasoning and gives enough evidence to support your conclusions and recommendations. The Discussion covers all of the above in more detail, plus possibly,

Pros and cons.
Intended results.
Critical success factors.
Alternative solutions.
Cost breakdown.
Process analysis.
Implementation schedule.
Resource requirements.
Vendor analysis.
Job plan.

Workplace Application—Technical Proposal

The following Quality Improvement Proposal illustrates another very simple format. It can be summarized as:

> **Proposal**—Brief summary of technical change requested and benefits to company.
> **Current environment**—What the current practices are.
> **Proposed change**—What actions are required and at what cost.
> **Benefits**—What business results justify the change, especially the financial implications.

Notice that logical organization makes even the most technical information clear. With the main idea up front and sections clearly focused with informative headings, even a lay reader understands the big picture.

To: Internal Client

From: I.M. Analyst

Date: June 7, 200__

Subject: Proposal to Purchase Modems to Reduce Costs

Quality Improvement Proposal

By replacing five 4800 bps modems on monthly rental from BIG PHONE with 56 Kbps modems, we can eliminate lease costs, improve response time, reduce file transfer times (thereby reducing connect-time costs) and better manage the lines required for mainframe dial access by Coal and Petroleum.

Current Environment

- Three lines reserved for dial access by the two mines and the two refineries.
- Two BIG PHONE modems on rent (cost for one modem not found in known BIG PHONE bills) for $294 at Corporate and one each at Mine 1 and Mine 2 for $288.00 per month (total of $582.00).
- One line dedicated for dial-up access at 28 Kbps (ideally should be two) by the Central Region and Mine 1 System/6000 computers as back-up for the X.25 mainframe access to the mainframe.
- A decision has been made to delay installation of the East Kentucky System/6000 until 200__.

Proposed Change

- Purchase three 56K modems (one 14.4K modem has already been purchased by Coal) at a cost of $2,100.00 for Corporate.

Quality improvement proposal

- Create a pool of four 56K modems for access by the mines, Central Region, and refineries.

- Have the four sites purchase 56 Kbps modems for a total of $2,800.00 (i.e., 4 modems at $700.00 each). Central Region and Mine 1 have compatible 28 Kbps modems and could retain those if desired.

Benefits/Justification

- Reduce monthly BIG PHONE rentals by $582.00.

- Payout for the modem purchases (a total of $4,900.00) is nine months if the refineries purchase new modems.

- Payout for the modem purchases is six months if the refineries can locate comparable modems already on-hand.

- Decrease on-line response times by nearly two-thirds (e.g., if response time is 6 seconds, a response time of 2–3 seconds can be expected).

- Decrease file transfer time by nearly two-thirds, reducing long distance cost (when connection is primarily for file transfer).

- Improve availability of dial access for the affected locations and potentially reduce total number of lines required.

- Standardization of SDLC dial access at 56 Kbps using the V.32bis modulation standard.

YOUR TURN

Developing a Proposal

Purpose: Your employer is considering a new performance appraisal policy. In the past, raises were granted based on seniority. The new system would create annual performance reviews, with salary increases tied to those reviews. You have been asked to serve on an employee task force to consider the benefits of such a policy and to propose a plan of action to Mr. Fuller, the manager of Human Resources. Although he is not actively opposed to the change, he has been with the organization for years and likes the current seniority system.

In planning, consider such questions as these:

> What are the problems with the current system?
> What are the pros and cons associated with a change?
> What solution(s) do you recommend?

> What benefits does your solution offer?
> What specific actions are necessary to implement a new system (e.g., supervisor-employee meetings, new forms, training)?
> What timetable would you suggest?

Take some time to brainstorm ideas to include in your proposal. Then evaluate those ideas and organize them into a working outline for the proposal. Remember to consider your audiences and purpose as you shape your blueprint. ■

Justifying Your Point

In simple proposals, you do not need to analyze pros and cons extensively. You only need to justify the idea you are proposing. In that case, organize details into:

> Your point—what you want to change.
> Your reasons—why the change is beneficial.
> The action requested—what you want your readers to do.

The following e-mail, "Justifying Your Point," exemplifies this model.

Workplace Application—Justifying a Change

From: Sam Manager
To: Ed Supervisor
Date: Mon., June 21, 200_
Subject: NEW REPORTING HOURS

Eddie,

Let's consider changing our hours to 6:00 a.m. until 2:30 p.m. This will enable us to accomplish several things. Of course, beating some of the afternoon heat is the main consideration, but it will also help to avoid a lot of the morning traffic by having the crews out of the yard no later than 6:30. I think too that we will see less conflict between the public and the trim crews, especially around park spray pools and shelters. Give this some consideration, and let me know what you decide. We will need a letter informing the employees affected.

Justifying your point

Would this e-mail be even clearer if broken into three paragraphs? If so, where would you divide it?

Requesting a Change

Purpose: Write an e-mail to your supervisor requesting a change in office procedure or permission to purchase a piece of equipment.   ■

Conveying 5 Ws and H Information

Sometimes your sole purpose is to convey information about something: announcing a decision, setting a meeting, reporting on a trip. In that case, brainstorm your ideas with the 5 Ws and H of the newspaper reporter: Who, What, When, Where, Why, and How.

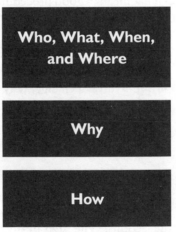

Ws and H information

Using a Problem-Solving Strategy

While your purpose sometimes is strictly to convey information, most business writing is persuasive. Using a problem-solving strategy sells the readers your idea clearly and effectively. In fact, most workplace documents—reports, proposals, letters, memos, and e-mail—are written to solve problems.

The complexity of your writing task determines the specific information in each section. For example, in the report format the Overview covers the problem (business context) and solution (conclusions and recommendations). For very short memos, e-mails, and letters, you may need only a few paragraphs.

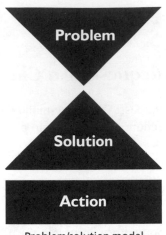

Problem/solution model

Explaining a Procedure

When you explain how to do something, always assume that you have inexperienced readers. Why would someone read a procedure carefully if he or she already knew what to do? That means a good procedure will orient the readers *up front* about six possible Ws.

An experienced consultant tells about reviewing a three-page procedure written for a municipal water plant. The first sentence said, "Flip Switch A." Three pages later, at the end of the procedure, came this warning: "Note: You must work quickly. When you flip Switch A, you turn off power to the plant."

What's wrong with this picture?

1. **What** the procedure achieves or why it is important.
2. **Who** is responsible for the procedure?
3. If it involves a change, **why** the change was made.
4. **When** it applies.
5. **What** equipment, materials, and manuals to gather.
6. Any **warnings** or special notes.

The traditional procedure resembles a story: Here is how this process works. However, modern procedures look more like a script: Who is the actor and what are the actions? The step-by-step explanation uses the Actor/Act details you brainstormed in planning if more than one person is involved. Identify the actors and action steps in chronological order, renaming each actor when responsibility shifts.

Both experienced readers and novices need clear headings to help them find the particular information they seek. The steps themselves should be action-oriented. Of course, the procedure must be complete.

During a patient's two-week follow-up appointment with his cardiologist, he informed his doctor that he was having trouble with one of his medications. "Which one?" the doctor asked. "The patch. The nurse told me to put on a new one every six hours, and now I'm running out of places to put it!" The doctor had him quickly undress and discovered what she hoped she wouldn't see. . . . Yes, the man had over 50 patches on his body! Now the instructions include removal of the old patch before applying a new one.

Writing Action-Oriented Procedures

Passive verbs in the traditional procedure style pose a major danger of ambiguity. The lack of an "actor" makes unclear who is responsible for doing the action. (See Chapter 5, "Editing," for a more thorough discussion of passive verbs.)

Instead of Passive:　　"The following changes **need to be made**."
　　　　　　　　　　　　　　　　　　　　　passive
　　　　　　　　　　　By whom?

Try Active:　　"Please **make** the following changes."
　　　　　　　　　　　active

Passives add unnecessary words, create a low-impact voice, and mask responsibility; the active style is concise, energetic, and clear.

Workplace Application—Action-Oriented Procedures

The following before and after procedure requests illustrate how clarity increased when the writer chose an active style.

To:　　Robert Peters
From:　Betty Dean
Date:　October 18, 200__
Re:　　Change to Percent Current Production Reports

As you may remember from the meeting we had with K. C. Smith, some changes need to be made to this report.

Original procedure

For Coal only, a separate report should be created for customers "00011," "00022," and "00033"; and these customers excluded from the primary report. The new report should be titled "Percent Current—Voluntary Pay Customers."

For all segments, the negative balances being excluded from the main reports should now be included and the separate totalling for them in the "unadjusted totals" should be eliminated. All segments will need a month-end version to be run on the 7th or 8th work nights. This version will need to incorporate any items on the closed item file which were still open on the last day of the month.

I don't know if Treasury still wants the Friday night version currently in production—check out with K. C. Smith or David Case.

To: Robert Peters

From: Betty Dean

Date: October 18, 200__

Re: **Change to Percent Current Production Reports**

As we discussed in our meeting with K. C. Smith, please make the following changes to the Percent Current reports:

- For Coal only, create a separate report for customers "00011," "00022," and "00033." Title the new report "Percent Current—Voluntary Pay Customers." Then exclude those customers from the primary report.

- For all segments, change the reports so that they no longer exclude negative balances. When you make this change, you will not need that coding which creates the "unadjusted totals." Take it out.

- Set up a month-end version of the report to run on the seventh or eighth work night. Add any invoices to this report from the closed item file which were still open on the last day of the month. Create an extract file similar to the one you did for the month-end aging reports to add to these items.

Once you've made these changes, it would probably be a good idea to ask K. C. Smith and David Case if they still want Friday night production runs for these reports. My guess is they will not.

cc: Barbara Fowler
    Dale Jones
    K.C. Smith
    David Case
    Jason Mason

Revised procedure

Modernizing Your Letters

Letters, by tradition, are the most formal type of document because they go to outsiders—customers, regulators, vendors, and business associates. Unfortunately, the formal tradition has often frozen both the format and the style of letters in the 20th century. Changes in the modern workplace—in technology (computers, fax) and in audience (unknown addressees and gender)—now dictate a more contemporary style. The following letter is an example of outdated format and style—and it is not very clear.

Workplace Application—Outdated versus Modern Style

March 3, 200__

County Courthouse
500 South Denver
City, State 94103

Attention: County Assessor

Gentlemen:

Please provide me with the information of whether or not you assess ad valorem taxes on the following types of properties in your county:

Mineral Producing   _____

Mineral Non-Producing _____

Please return this information in the enclosed self-addressed, postage-paid envelope.

Sincerely,

George W. Smith

George W. Smith
Tax Department

GWS/bg
Enclosure

Outdated letter style

March 3, 200__

County Courthouse
500 South Denver
City, ST 94103

Attention: County Assessor

Do you assess ad valorem taxes on the following types of properties in your county?

    Mineral Producing   _____

    Nonmineral Producing _____

Please return this information in the enclosed envelope, or fax it to 909-555-4321. Thank you for your help.

George W. Smith

George W. Smith
Tax Department

GWS/bg
enclosure

Modern letter style

Is the simplified version of the same letter appropriate and clear? If so, why? What has changed?

In modern letter style, you may:

> Use full block paragraphs and page layout (no indentations) for a more readable format. In addition, studies show that a left-justified and ragged right margin is more readable than a fully justified margin. Spreading the letters to fully justify text reduces readability.

> Replace the salutation with an attention line, especially if the letter serves the same purpose as an office-to-office memo or if you do not know the gender of the addressee.

> Omit the complimentary close if you omit the salutation.

> Omit courtesy titles (Mr., Mrs., and Ms.) in the address lines, except for formal occasions. If you use a title, Ms. is generally accepted for females, but follow the addressee's preference. Indicate professional titles either by placing the degree abbreviation after the name or by using Dr. before the name.

> Use a comma instead of a colon in a personal business letter salutation.
> Ask direct questions.
> Use headings and bulleted lists to make text more readable.
> Use *you, I,* and *we.* Personal pronouns give letters a warm, human voice.

YOUR TURN

Responding to an Angry Former Customer

The customer service group of a regional bank's credit card division received the following letter.

Gentlemen:

Enclosed please find my check for 48.86 which will pay my bill in full less the following deductions.

Interested Charge	7.48
	12.00
	19.40

Since you were so nice to cancel my card for no reason or at least you could of issue me another under another number without the statement your card has been cancelled. I feel I am entitled to at least 3/4 of my fee I paid you for the use of your card for a year. In addition to that I feel you took the auto club for a ride just to increase your card business. *Dirty Pool I Call it.* Furthermore I considered it a reflection on my credit when you cancelled my card. You have always been paid in full way ahead of the due date except this last time which was a slip in my book-keeping. My credit is more important to me than anything else. In fact that is why my wife and I got a devorce but it was not over a charge accont but a lot bigger sum on a business.

I am still considering haveing a class mate which is a lawyer file a suit against you. I may not win but it dam sure cost you some money. I am expecting a letter from you.

Sincerly,

George Hotunderthecollar

Angry customer letter

Mr. Hotunderthecollar was correct. He did have a good credit rating and did not deserve to have his card cancelled, based on his payment record.

However, the bank had to cancel his card because of the divorce. The original account was for both parties, and bank policy required canceling any jointly held accounts. In addition, the card had been issued through an agreement with the auto club, a contract that was expiring. The auto club prohibited the bank from soliciting new accounts from former cardholders, so the bank could not offer to open a new account under the gentleman's own name.

Unfortunately, when Mr. Hotunderthecollar wrote to drop his ex-wife's name from the account, no one explained the situation to him. He simply received a cancellation notice plus interest due.

Mr. Hotunderthecollar is "expecting a letter." In responding, brainstorm details you might want to include, organize your points, and then write a draft. Be sure to arrange points based on what is important to Mr. Hotunderthecollar.

Communicating Electronically

E-mail is replacing memos and letters. Traditionally, a letter was a formal communication with external audiences; memos were less formal because they reached internal audiences. New technology has destroyed those distinctions. E-mail and fax—new *delivery* methods—routinely zap messages to both internal and external readers.

Despite this pervasive usage, e-mail is perceived to be an extremely informal medium, almost like a personal conversation, which may lack clear organization, verbal precision, or grammatical care. For personal e-mail between friends, such a conversational tone may be okay. But for a business e-mail, the result can be a decidedly reader-unfriendly—and unprofessional—message.

Consider the advantages and disadvantages of e-mail shown in Table 3-1.

TABLE 3-1. Advantages and Disadvantages of E-mail

Advantages	Disadvantages
• Convenient, quick	• "Dirty"—grammar errors and rambling
• Get instant answers	• Delayed (or unknown) responses
• Can easily send multiple copies	• Junk mail
• References are attached	• Scavenger hunts or bad "chain letters"
• Can access any time and place	• NOT private
• Saves paper	• Have a life of their own
• Low cost	• Legally binding
• Documented (written, permanent)	• Hard to erase
• Encourages teamwork	• Hard to find for later reference
• Gives you time to cool off	• Lose tone of voice and personality

Ferris Research estimates the overall benefit of e-mail "in terms of increased productivity equals about $9,000 per employee." —Dan Dieterich Communication Consultant	"It's as ubiquitous as winter damp, a pernicious miasma that brings rot and ruin to society's delicate underpinnings. I speak of e-mail, the greatest threat to civilization since lead dinnerware addled the brains of the Roman aristocracy." —Seth Shostak *Newsweek*

"E-mail is a stack of dynamite with your name on it."

—Unknown

Maximizing E-mail

To improve your electronic communication, follow these guidelines:

Manage the medium.

> *Choose your medium wisely.* Is it better to call or write? Is e-mail, which is an impersonal medium, the best way to achieve the result you want? Should you call instead, for example, regarding personnel matters, changing an agreement, or establishing a time frame? Or should you write a letter or memorandum?

> *Send less.* Everyone is buried in information these days. Send only messages that count (e.g., do not thank someone for thanking you!).

> *Target your distribution list.* People stop reading when they receive too many messages. Include only those readers who need your message. "Fan-out messages" waste everyone's time.

> *Establish organizational guidelines.* Determine as an organization what type of messages are appropriate. Do you want employees to use e-mail for personal business, telling jokes, advertising their garage sales, or selling charity raffle tickets? Violating e-mail policy may be grounds for termination.

Treat e-mail as a "real" document.

> *Use principles of good writing.* Plan, organize, edit, and refine. Focus on meeting your audiences' needs for information, style, and clarity.

> *Think before you write.* E-mail is *not* a conversation. You should treat it like any written document by planning and organizing before you write. Remember: E-mail has all the legal standing of any written document. Plus, it goes farther, faster, to more people.

> *Get to the point.* The first paragraph should tell your readers the point you are making. Your subject line should cover the point. Readers may not open the document if the subject line is not clearly focused.

> *Be diplomatic.* Because e-mail seems like a conversation, we can respond too quickly. We sometimes write things that tone of voice or humor would soften, but on the cold, hard screen sound inappropriate or rude. Cool off before you respond and then have damage to control.

> *Follow standard capitalization rules.* Typing in all capitals is perceived as shouting; all lowercase is poetic but improper. Both are hard to read and invite more punctuation errors.

> *Proofread.* E-mail should be quick but not dirty. If you overlook spelling and punctuation errors, if you don't care about sentence structure, your readers have to translate. Reader-friendly writing—even electronically—requires the courtesy of quality control.

All messages going outside the organization—regardless of whether the messages are in paper or e-mail form—should therefore be treated as if they were official organization records and conform to a specified writing standard—addressing content, type of language, use of slang, grammar and spelling requirements, review, etc. This writing standard would also be appropriate for all official records only maintained internally."

DONALD S. SKUPSKY

Focusing E-mail

Purpose: The following e-mail is complete but indirect. Without a clear main idea and strong key points, readers will have to figure out the writer's point. Reorganize the e-mail using one of the organizational models discussed in this chapter: proposal, point/reasons, or problem/solution/action. Then rewrite the e-mail. Remember to focus the subject line.

To: George Johnson

From: Sam Simpson

Cc: Robert Martin, David Whitman, Matt Jones, George James

Subject: Carlin Conduits

George, I spoke with Matt and Gary Winston today. Gary said the electrical contractor suggested that when the building is moved, they leave all those conduits there and make a large junction box there and reuse some of those old conduits.

I would like to express my opinion on this matter, if you are considering this change. When I first looked at this project I thought that would be what we could do but, after giving some thought to it, I remembered all those conduits out there surrounding the building! There are TONS of conduits around that building! Some of these conduits are hard to identify. There have been so many conduits installed over the years so close to each other and running every which way, that reusing these will compound the problem. I think it would be advantageous to tear out many of those and run new, in a logical uncrowded manner. In the future, there will be no question a) which conduit b) exactly how it's routed c) where it is d) if Gary is the inspector, he will know within inches where someone can dig or set something. e) New wire will be multi-conductor cable whereas, most of those old conduits contain single conductor and could be too small.

The difference in price will be worth it with ease of identity and orderly routing.

Can you tell which way I'm leaning?
Thanks,
Sam

Indirect message

Designing Your Document

New technology allows us to produce more readable documents, *if* we think beyond our traditional concepts of what text looks like. It is still important to organize ideas and details logically in a well-focused blueprint. Then we can add an architecture, making the shape of the document clear. Studies show that headings, white space with lists, and even side-by-side text can make documents far more reader-friendly.

Workplace Application—Document Design

The following original and redesigned memos illustrate the importance of document design. The original memo, developed to control high turnover and improve employee reliability, was complete and logically organized. Employees received it as part of their new employee orientation. However, notice how much more reader-friendly the redesigned version is.

Analyze the original and redesigned versions by answering these questions:

> How do you think employees responded to the original?
> What are the key points it makes?
> What did the writer change to improve readability in the redesigned version?
> What stands out?
> How could employees use the redesigned version?

Maintenance Division

TO: New Maintenance Employee

FROM: Sam Smithson
            Superintendent

SUBJECT: Expectations and Responsibilities

As the successful applicant for this position, we welcome you to the Maintenance Division!

There are some very important expectations and responsibilities associated with this position that we want to share with you. Your overall attendance (sick leave, AWOL's, tardies, LWOP's) needs to be maintained at an acceptable level as required

---

Original memo

Organizing

in the Division policies. Good attendance is critical because the Maintenance Division is responsible for emergency services to citizens in the City. The entire section must respond to these calls as quickly as possible, and your absence may affect getting the job completed quickly and efficiently. Failure to maintain good attendance during your probationary period will result in your immediate termination.

In order to successfully complete the six-month probationary period and maintain your position in this Division, you must have good attendance and be performing all of your job duties at a satisfactory level by the end of the six months probation. Service Writer, Master Mechanics, Mechanics, and Mechanic Helpers must also obtain a Class "A" Commercial Driver's License.

It is extremely important that you follow supervisory instructions and display a cooperative, positive attitude at all times while conducting City business, including in your offices, in training sessions or any portion of the office complex. You will be expected to conduct yourself in a professional manner when interacting with other employees, your supervisors, citizens and vendors—treating everyone with dignity and respect.

You must perform your job, not only effectively and efficiently, but **safely**. Following safe working procedures is a **job requirement**. A high percentage of accidents and job injuries are a result of employees violating common safety practices and procedures. Accidents and/or injuries could be reduced or eliminated by employees simply understanding the importance of practicing safety both on and off the job. Because accidents and injuries add substantially to the cost of delivering services to our citizens, they must be kept to a minimum.

Congratulations on your new position in our organization, and we are confident you will enjoy a successful career in the Maintenance Division.

_____ Date _____
Employee Signature

_____ Date _____
Witness Signature

Maintenance Division

To: New Maintenance Employee

From: Sam Smithson, Superintendent

Subject: Expectations and Responsibilities

Welcome to Maintenance! Some very important responsibilities are associated with your position.

Probationary Requirements

To successfully complete the six-month probationary period and keep your position in this Division, you must:

- Maintain your overall attendance (sick leave, AWOLs, LWOPs, tardies) at the satisfactory level defined in the Division policies. During your probation, unsatisfactory attendance will result in immediate termination.

- Perform all job duties at a satisfactory level by the end of the six months.

- Service Writer, Master Mechanics, Mechanics, and Mechanic Helpers **must** also acquire and maintain a Class "A" Commercial Driver's License.

Personal Conduct

You must follow supervisory instructions and display a cooperative, positive attitude while conducting City business, including in City offices and vehicles, in training sessions, or in any portion of the office complex. When interacting with other employees, your supervisors, citizens and vendors, conduct yourself in a professional manner—treating everyone with dignity and respect.

Safety

Violating safety practices and procedures causes accidents and job injuries which add substantially to the cost of delivering services to our citizens. By following City and Division safety policies, you can perform your job effectively, efficiently, and **safely**.

Congratulations on your new position in our organization, and we are confident you will enjoy a successful career in the Maintenance Division.

_____ Date _____
Employee Signature

_____ Date _____
Witness Signature

Redesigned memo

Graphics Tips for Creating Readable Documents

Good document design follows the KIS principle—Keep It Simple! Follow these guidelines in using the design elements that new technology provides:

Fonts

> Use serif fonts such as Times New Roman, Garamond, or Palatino Linotype for continuous text. According to studies, the horizontal elements at the base of the letters carry the reader's eyes forward, linking the words.

> Use sans serif fonts such as Arial, **Tahoma**, or Verdana for headings. The unfooted style emphasizes a free-standing element.

> Limit the number of font types on a page to three.

> Avoid casual fonts like **Comic Sans** or *Monotype Corsiva* in professional documents.

> Prefer moderately weighted fonts such as Times New Roman. A thick font like **Impact** or a thin font like MS Mincho are hard to read.

> Choose a font size from 10 to 12 points for text and larger for headings.

Emphasis

> Emphasize words by using **bold**, *italics,* or color.

> Avoid underlining and ALL CAPS, which interfere with reading.

Layout

> Use full block style, with all text elements left-justified and no paragraph indentation.

> Choose symbols to mark lists that are appropriate to their content.

> Use numbered lists if you are enumerating or presenting a chronological sequence.

> Use bulleted lists to indicate like items or ideas, usually in descending order of importance.

> Make lists parallel in structure—that is, all phrases, all action statements, or all sentences.

> Avoid inappropriate background templates—for example, in e-mail. They are unprofessional looking and take longer to download.

Organizing

Chapter 3 focused on how to better organize your writing. This chapter explained the following points:

> You learned about strategies that will help you organize a wide variety of writing tasks.

> You were introduced to the five questions you need to ask yourself when organizing your writing.

> You learned about 5Ws and H, problem-solution, and actor/act as organizing tools.

> You saw the importance of professionalism when writing letters and e-mail.

> You added document design as an important feature of clear writing. ■

Writing

Potential Problems	Strategies
Paragraph covers more than one topic.	Write strong, controlling topic sentences.
	Limit each paragraph to one key point and supporting details.
Paragraph is not arranged logically.	Plan paragraphs before you write by:
	• Jotting down the details.
	• Arranging points in logical order and adding transitions.
	• Placing your topic sentence at the beginning of the paragraph.
Paragraph requires too much concentration to follow.	Use visual clues such as headings and lists.
Relationship of one paragraph to the next is not clear.	Connect paragraphs with standard transitions and paragraph hooks.
Document is text-heavy.	Use graphics if they convey details more clearly than words do.

Writing

Chapter 4

>>>>>>>

Writing

Writing

Writing the Document

Have you ever struggled through a document, feeling lost and frustrated, working hard to understand it by reading and then rereading? Wandering paragraphs, buried points, lack of logical direction, dense text—these symptoms of poor organization mean the writer expects the reader to create meaning out of raw information.

> The skill of writing is to create a context in which other people can think.
>
> EDWIN SCHLOSSBERG

But it's the writer's job to do the thinking. Having organized your ideas into a high-level map, you focus on writing the draft—filling in your general design with details. Some experts encourage students to freewrite to discover their ideas while they create text. That approach works if you need a topic for an essay, but in the workplace you generally know your topic. Brainstorming first, then writing from a well-designed map is usually more efficient than writing to discover.

This chapter completes the answer to "What Are My Key Points?"—the logical development of key points in paragraphs. Even though this is a very basic subject, poorly focused paragraphs can be a serious problem. Without organization, key points are buried or omitted. Then interested readers must search for points and may misinterpret data; disinterested readers stop reading. Writing clear paragraphs allows your readers to find information efficiently.

Well-written paragraphs depend on:

> Understanding the relationship of specific details to more abstract concepts.
> Developing strong topic sentences that clarify key points.
> Focusing on one key point per paragraph.
> Creating a logical flow so that readers stay on track.
> Integrating text and visuals when a graphic will be more reader-friendly.

The Ladder of Abstraction

The English language contains a wide spectrum of terms for any given thing, ranging from very concrete, specific, visual terms such as *cow* through gradually more general and abstract terms like *livestock, farm assets,* and *resources.* The Ladder of Abstraction, a concept popularized by S. I. Hayakawa in *Language in Thought and Action,* helps us understand both how language works and how to use it to write well. This ladder shows that effective communication depends on clearly relating words to the things, people, or ideas they represent.

The example of the word *profit* in Figure 4-1 follows the progression from the object itself to concrete/specific terms to abstract words, moving from the bottom *up* the ladder.

The process of abstracting, a crucial human ability to think and speak in more general terms, involves noting similarities and ignoring differences. Humans need to communicate in general terms, to be able to group ideas or products or persons. We could not analyze "profits" or "programs" or "personnel" without the ability to abstract.

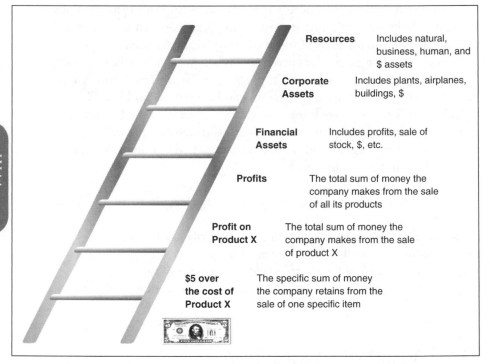

Resources	Includes natural, business, human, and $ assets
Corporate Assets	Includes plants, airplanes, buildings, $
Financial Assets	Includes profits, sale of stock, $, etc.
Profits	The total sum of money the company makes from the sale of all its products
Profit on Product X	The total sum of money the company makes from the sale of product X
$5 over the cost of Product X	The specific sum of money the company retains from the sale of one specific item

Figure 4-1: The Ladder of Abstraction.
Source: Adapted from S. I. Hayakawa, Language in Thought and Action, *4th edition (Boston: Heinle, 1978). Copyright 1978 by Heinle, a division of Thomson Learning. Reprinted with permission.*

Getting a Bit Too Abstract

The risk of abstracting involves choosing content or words that don't really stand for anything. Sometimes the temptation to use fancy words creates fog, not meaning. High-level abstractions may sound good, but vague writing does not impress anyone. And it does not communicate. If you find yourself writing in circles, ask yourself:

> ➤ What am I *really* trying to say?
> ➤ Do I need to give a concrete example?
> ➤ Is there a more specific word I could use?

Using the Ladder to Organize

The Ladder of Abstraction reveals the tendency of some writers and speakers to get stuck at one level. This dead-level abstracting sometimes occurs at a low level: A writer who presents only data without ever generalizing or drawing conclusions leaves readers wondering, "What is the point?" Dead-level abstracting also occurs at a high level, in the clouds of abstract thinking. *Theories, strategies, planning, vision,* and *goals* are meaningful words only when tied to the specifics they represent.

Thus, the issue is not whether we should use abstractions. We must. The issue, instead, concerns *how* we use abstractions. Effective writing moves freely up and down the Ladder, presenting abstract statements as the main idea and key points and then supporting them with specific evidence, examples, and explanation.

Using the Ladder to Edit

The Ladder of Abstraction also gives insights into developing a clear style. Good writers choose specific or concrete words as low on the ladder as possible. For example,

> ➤ "A profit of $5 per widget" is more precise than "a good profit."
> ➤ "A bus that seats 32 people" is clearer than "adequate transportation."
> ➤ "Please respond before March 1" is more accurate than "Please respond at your earliest convenience."

The Ladder of Abstraction reminds you to decide, "How much detail should I include so that my readers understand?" and "What words should I choose to be clear?"

Writing Paragraphs

A paragraph is a group of sentences that fully explain one idea so that your readers clearly understand both your reasoning and the evidence that supports that reasoning. To accomplish this purpose, a fully developed paragraph has two parts:

1. A strong topic sentence that states your general key point.
2. Logically arranged details, or specific evidence, that fully explain the key point.

Deciding How Long a Paragraph Should Be

There is no rule governing paragraph length. To completely explain a key point, a standard paragraph usually contains between 50 and 150 words. However, paragraphs in short letters, memos, and e-mails with very limited topics may be shorter. But very short paragraphs (one or two sentences each) suggest that the key point has not been fully explained. On the other hand, a paragraph that is too long may not clearly focus on just one topic. You should consider dividing paragraphs that are too long or unfocused to give each key point the attention it deserves and sometimes simply to give the reader's eye a rest.

One wag suggested, "A paragraph should be like a woman's skirt: long enough to cover the topic, but short enough to be interesting."

Focusing Key Points in Topic Sentences

A strong topic sentence is the key to effective paragraphing. It tells the reader what to expect in the rest of the paragraph. However, it is not enough to say, "The next topic is the use of computers in the workplace." A good topic sentence names both the *topic* and your *point* about that topic; it focuses and directs the paragraph. Therefore, each topic sentence should identify both your topic and your point (or controlling idea) about that topic.

For example:

> *Topic (T)*   *Point (P)*
> **Computers** are now **essential** to American industry.

Readers expect to find the topic sentence at the beginning of the paragraph. We tend to think inductively: Gather data and then draw a conclusion or point. If we write that way, the topic sentence shows up at the end of the paragraph. But readers generally do not want to think with the writer. They prefer a deductive, point-first structure.

Workplace Application—Good Topic Sentences

Notice how the topic sentences clearly direct the following two paragraphs.

Business Example

                               P   *T*

The team has determined that **no further reduction** of **paperwork** is possible at the present growth rate (see attached report). Other actions anticipated to further reduce the amount of paperwork are being investigated by other teams; therefore, the Quality Council recommended that this team be closed. Susan will continue to monitor copier usage for the next few months to evaluate the cause of any trends that may occur. Changes will be reported to Miguel Ordonez for action as necessary.

Technical Example

         T   *P*

The **installation** of Shadowing is rather **painless**. It requires loading the software onto the system, running Systemware's installation programs, and doing an update to the system from an SLT tape created during the installation process. The one drawback is that it has to be performed with no one accessing the system. You also have the support and backing of the support personnel 24 hours a day in the event that problems do occur with the installation. I have already installed a demo copy of this software on the system and had no problems doing the installation.

Topic Sentences

Purpose: The following sentences give you an opportunity to identify the key elements of a strong topic sentence. Underline and label the **topic** and **point** words in these sentences.   *T*   *P*

1. In the meeting, we will set guidelines for making our group more efficient.

2. The new vacation schedule is more practical than the old one.

3. The last project illustrates the problems created by the meddling of EMA investigators.

4. The tasks of this position can be grouped into three categories: administrative, clerical, and bookkeeping.

5. We must choose between two types of laboratory equipment. ■

Readers usually are more interested in what you *learned* than in what you did. The following paragraphs are narratives of what happened. Storytelling is appropriate for some paragraphs, such as a background section. However, focusing on a sequence of events can bury or omit the key point.

Buried Topic Sentences

Purpose: Move the buried topic sentence or create a topic sentence for each of the following paragraphs. Your goal is to put the *key point* up front.

1. On February 1, 1994, I performed air monitoring tests in the engine room at the Fareview station. The reason for the air monitoring was

to identify any presence of an organic vapor. I used a device called PHOAC—Photo Detector Model. It measures organic vapor in ppm, parts per million. I took sixteen separate readings in various areas in the engine, with the concentration on the Allo units. At the time of the testing, both units were operating. If there were a time when any organic vapors would be released, it should be when the units are operating. (Attached is a plot plan of the performed testing.) The results of the testing showed **absolutely no readings** of organic vapors in the engine room.

2. A tally of telephone calls inquiring into job openings was kept over a 1-month time period. It is estimated that approximately 1 to 1½ hours per day is spent on the telephone in response to these inquiries. The "job line" would allow Personnel employees to concentrate more of their time and efforts in other areas of the employment process. Southwest Energy, General Maintenance, and Advanced Equipment Company are a few of the major employers who utilize a job line to list job openings.

3. Currently deal sheets are filled out by hand by the traders and then given to the contract administrator. The contract administrator enters the data into a database and then deal reports are generated and given to the other users of the information who reenter the information for their applications. The same information gets keyed five or six times. ■

Creating Paragraph Unity

A strong topic sentence forces you to stick to the topic by clearly focusing on the key point. This focus is called *paragraph unity*. That means that all elements of the paragraph work together to explain one idea.

TIPS

An effective paragraph includes all relevant information, but leaves out unrelated details, no matter how interesting they may be. ■

Workplace Application—Paragraph Focus

How does this paragraph wander from the key point?

> The filing method in which five trays were removed appeared to be inefficient and counterproductive. In an effort to substantiate or refute the employee's claim, two samples were taken during the productivity survey. Again, during the first week, trays were left in the machines, while during the second week trays were removed.

Workplace Application—Choppy Paragraphs

You should also avoid a series of one sentence paragraphs, such as those in the following letter. Which sentences could be combined in paragraphs?

> Dear Engineer:
>
> This letter is in reference to your request for a copy of the atlas.
>
> Your request has been approved by Supervisor and has been forwarded to Reproduction. A copy of the atlas will be delivered to your location within two weeks.
>
> Your office will be added to our distribution list and updates will be sent to you accordingly.
>
> If you have any questions, please call me at extension _____ .
>
> Sincerely,
>
> Chief Draftsman

Imagine that you've been asked to pick up some important information in Bug Tussle this afternoon. You agree, but then discover there's no map to Bug Tussle and they've taken down all the road signs. You do know to head north.

You probably face a long afternoon—getting lost, stopping for directions, taking wrong turns, growing more and more frustrated. At best, the trip takes longer than it should. At worst, you give up and head home.

Your readers face the same frustration if you send them on an "information journey" without a good map and clear road signs along the way. Lost in detail, they may decide not to read at all. If they do finish the journey, you've wasted their time.

Drawing a complete map with good transitions is critical. You can't tell someone how to find Bug Tussle until you know where it is yourself.

Making Paragraphs Flow

Effective paragraphs are also coherent, or orderly, so that one sentence flows logically into the next. You create this flow in four ways.

1. Arrange details in *logical order*.
2. Add clear *transitions* from one sentence to the next.
3. Include *echo words,* or repetitions of certain important words to reinforce the key point.
4. Create a *logical chain* of sentences by moving the reader from old knowledge (known) to new information.

Logical Order

Common sense usually determines the arrangement of details. The following are common patterns.

> From *general to specific:* for example, applying a point of law to a specific case.
> From *specific to general:* for example, presenting scientific data before drawing the conclusion. This arrangement can put your topic sentence at the end of the paragraph.

> In *chronological order:* for example, describing a method of investigation or a history of events.
> In *visual order:* for example, describing some machinery.
> From *least important to most important:* for example, identifying or explaining reasons to justify a decision. This traditional approach assumes that readers will remember the last point best and that they read the entire paragraph or document.
> From *most important to least important:* for example, outlining the reasons to accept a proposal or to buy a product. Most workplace readers prefer this order because it focuses on their key concerns first.

As a general rule, the first and last positions—whether in a sentence, a paragraph, or a document—are the strongest and most remembered.

Transitions

To help your reader follow your logical direction, you must supply the road signs, or transitions from one sentence to the next. Transitional words and phrases show how the details in the paragraph relate. Some frequently used transitions include:

Addition:	also, too, again, in addition, next, finally, last
Comparison:	similarly, likewise, like, bulleted lists (•, •, •)
Contrast:	but, yet, however, still, on the other hand, on the contrary, otherwise
Enumeration:	first, second, third; 1, 2, 3, . . .
Illustration:	that is, i.e., for example, e.g., for instance
Place:	here, there, beyond, nearby, on the opposite side
Result:	therefore, thus, hence, as a result, consequently
Summary:	in other words, in fact, in summary, in short
Time:	immediately, then, soon, often, later, afterward

In addition, *personal pronouns,* such as he, she, it, they, and demonstrative pronouns, such as this, these, and that, are also transitions of a sort. They point backward to the noun they replace, linking the two in a continuous thought.

Claims Filing Procedure

Purpose: The following exercise tests your knowledge in analyzing the logical order and clear transitions of this procedure.

CLAIMS FILING PROCEDURE

Please read these instructions carefully before you present a claim. Effective use on your part of the information given below will ensure prompt processing of your claim. Your claim must be received by the Plan Administrator within 24 months from the date on which the expense was incurred. Failure to meet this deadline will prevent your claim from being reimbursed under the Plan.

Preparation of Your Bills

In preparing your bills, the following points should be considered:

First   Become familiar with eligible and ineligible expenses listed in this handbook.

Second Submit only the unaltered original (*not* a copy) of each bill. All bills must be itemized. Each bill should show:

     a. the name of the patient and the name and employee number of Employee;
     b. the nature of the illness or injury;
     c. the type of service or supply furnished;
     d. the date, or dates, that the service was rendered or the purchase was made;
     e. the charge for each service or supply;
     f. prescription drug bills will be handled under the provisions of the Prescription Drug Program (see p.1).

     Cancelled checks, cash register "receipts" and bills showing only a "balance forward" are not acceptable. All bills must be legible.

Third   Where convenient, bills should be accumulated until (1) treatment has been concluded and your claim is complete, or (2) treatment is continuing and the accumulated expenses represent a significant sum, at least equal to the deductible amount, if any.

Remember, claims submitted later than 24 months after the date the charges were incurred are ineligible.

Claims filing procedure

Writing

Echo Words

Echo words, or effective repetition of key words in a paragraph, reinforce the key point. This repetition, instead of being redundant, reminds the reader of the paragraph topic and the relevance of details. Notice the echoes in the paragraph presented next.

Workplace Application—Echoes

P　　　　T

There are **excellent sampling procedures** in place for final product. They run **extensive laboratory analyses** on samples from the test hopper in order to grade materials as prime or off-grade. **Additional sampling and testing** are conducted on the railcar retain **sample** at the time of shipment. Three compartments **are sampled** from each railcar for melt flow index, with one **analysis** run on each **sample**. **Additional tests** are also run on a composite **sample** from the railcar.

Of course, too many echoes can become redundant—saying the same thing several times. Be sure to use only relevant details and vary your word choice.

Logical Chain

Studies show that readers can follow even the most complex technical information more easily if sentences move from known information to new information. In other words, clearly organized paragraphs build a logical chain—one link at a time. Imagine this progression:

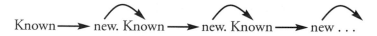

Known ⟶ new. Known ⟶ new. Known ⟶ new . . .

In the next paragraph, each sentence builds on the information presented in the sentence before.

Workplace Application—Logical Chain

I propose this well should be checked for scaling tendencies to determine **if some remedial work** should be performed to improve production. **If no remedial work** is indicated, temporary abandonment should be considered while **other options** are explored. **These options** include plug and abandonment, checking for other potential producing zones, or converting to a salt water disposal well to serve both the United and Excellent production areas.

Bringing Paragraphs Together

These same techniques—logical order, transitions, echoes, and logical chains—are also effective in creating links between paragraphs. Acting like hooks that connect railcars, these paragraph transitions are smooth when:

> The topic sentence clearly relates to and advances the main idea of the document.

> Standard transition words appear in the topic sentence to hook it to the preceding paragraph.

> Key words from the preceding paragraph are echoed in the topic sentence of the next.

Of course, to build such a logical structure, having a clear map is essential. Even a rough plan that you create before actually writing will help. Making ideas clear to your readers is impossible until *you* know what you are going to say.

Opening and Closing

The opening and closing paragraphs in any document are extremely important because they may be the only part of the document your readers read. Most people say they usually look at the first paragraph to learn what the document is about and the last paragraph to learn what to do and by when (see Figure 4-2).

Your opening paragraph should:	**Your closing paragraph should:**
• Identify the business issue or problem.	• Restate the main idea.
• State the purpose and/or main idea (solution).	• State the specific action to be taken and the due date, if possible.

Issue	I am responding to your search for a technical writer as advertised in the *Daily News*. . . .	**Main Idea**	Once you have have had an opportunity to review the enclosed resume, . . .
Purpose	This letter will summarize my background and qualifications.	**Action**	I will call next week to see if we can meet in person to further discuss my qualifications.
Problem	Eunice Matthews has sent me 37 different letters which Customer Service currently has set up on word processing.	**Main Idea**	I am now asking for your help in addressing the letters situation. . . .
Main Idea	This large number raises several concerns about consistency.	**Action**	By March 3, would each of you please prepare the following: . . .

Figure 4-2: Opening and closing paragraphs

Opening and Closing Style

Most writers rely on stock openings and closings to save time and to feel confident their style is appropriate. Try to avoid the tired phrases that often begin and end letters, memos, and e-mail messages. Instead, choose phrases with a modern, human voice.

Write openings that sound like a professional conversation.

Instead of the old-fashioned:	Try the modern:
Please be advised that your proposal has been approved.	Your proposal has been approved.
In reference to your letter dated . . .	Thank you for your January 6, 200__ letter.
This memo is in reply to your request . . .	As you requested, . . .
The purpose of this report is to analyze . . .	This report analyzes . . .
As per our telephone conversation . . .	As we discussed . . .
Enclosed please find a list of . . .	The enclosed list . . .
Herein attached is a spreadsheet . . .	The attached spreadsheet . . .
This will acknowledge your letter of . . .	We received your letter . . .
We regret (or are pleased) to inform you that . . .	Unfortunately . . . Congratulations . . .
In your letter dated June 17, it was stated . . .	Your June 17 letter stated . . .

Write closings that sound like a natural call to action.

Instead of:	Try:
Old-fashioned Hoping to hear from you in the affirmative, I am . . .	**Modern** I hope you agree to . . .
Cliché Enclosed you will find a self-addressed, stamped envelope for your convenience.	**Fresh** Please return the form in the enclosed envelope.
Negative Please do not hesitate to call.	**Positive** Please call . . .

Instead of:	Try:
Formal	**Natural**
Your cooperation in this matter will be greatly appreciated.	Thank you for your help.
Vague	**Precise**
Please respond at your earliest convenience.	Please return the form before June 1.

YOUR TURN

Revising Openings and Closings

Purpose: In this exercise, you will rewrite these openings and closings to be more concise and effective:

1. It has come to my attention that an overcharge was made in December on my account of $25.00.

_____

_____

_____

_____

2. We have referred your letter of November 15 to our Legal Department, and they have advised us that you are entitled to full coverage.

_____

_____

_____

_____

3. Thanks in advance for your cooperation in this request for more current statistics.

_____

_____

_____

_____

4. Your assistance in resolving this problem before December 31 is greatly appreciated.

_____

_____

_____

_____

5. As per our conversation of Monday, May 26, 200__, in regard to the aforementioned project, it is my wish that you proceed.

_____

_____

_____

_____

Creating Visual Clues

Traditional paragraph style creates a box—one sentence after another with either a five-space indentation or no indentation at the beginning. New technology allows us to create much more reader-friendly paragraphs.

> Open lists that look like an **I** or **T**
> Columns for comparisons
> Inserted graphics with meaty captions

These modern paragraphs still meet the traditional definition of a paragraph: "A paragraph is a group of sentences explaining one idea." However, they do so in a manner that pleases the eye and adds variety to the writing landscape.

Workplace Application—Traditional versus Open Layout

The open format in paragraphs helps readers grasp information more easily. The logical relationships then take shape, just as they did after a supervisor suggested revising the memo from the original to the revised, both of which follow. What did the writer change to improve clarity and readability?

Date: 12/16/0__

To: Manager

From: Maintenance Clerk

Subject: Kit Alternatives

The original Log Plan for the controller used 6 Regional offices for the Kit distribution centers due to the high cost of the Third Program stated below. The 6 Regional Kits would cost $_____ dollars. But, one exposure in regards to that plan was establishing only 6 sites for Kits would be insufficient saturation of spare parts in the field.

Attached are three alternative Kit distribution cost analyses. The first program would consist of 12 centers, located at key Air Freight Hub Distribution sites at a cost of $_____. Second program consists of 14 centers, located at _____ _____. To establish this program would be $_____. The third program is the most costly at $_____. They would be distributed to all 129 Service Centers forecasted in the Maintenance Plan.

Original memo—traditional paragraph layout

Date: 12/16/0__

To: Manager

From: Maintenance Clerk

Subject: Kit Alternatives

The original Log Plan for the controller used 6 Regional offices for the Kit distribution centers due to the high cost of the Third Program stated below in "Alternatives." But establishing only 6 sites for Kits could mean that not enough spare parts would reach the field.

Original Plan:

6 Regional kits = $

Alternatives:

First Program = $

Consists of 12 centers, located at Key Air Freight Hub Distribution sites.

Second Program = $

Consists of 14 centers, located at 6 Regional offices plus 8 additional Zones.

Third Program = $

Consists of all 129 Service Centers forecasted in the Maintenance Plan.

You will find attached cost analyses of the three Alternative programs for Kit distribution.

Revised memo—open paragraph layout

YOUR TURN

Paragraph Formatting

Purpose: In the following exercise you will practice reformatting a paragraph. Legal notices to consumers often pack as much information into a paragraph as possible. Besides being very reader-*unfriendly,* such notices seem designed to hide meaning. Reformat the disclosure clause that follows to open up the visually packed paragraph and clarify the terms of subscriber privacy.

DISCLOSURE. The Cable Act allows us to collect personally identifiable information and to disclose it to a third party only if (a) you consent in advance in writing or electronically; (b) disclosure is necessary to render cable service and other services we provide to you and related business activities; (c) disclosure is required pursuant to a court order and you are notified of such order; or (d) for mailing lists as described below. The Cable Act requires us to inform you of the nature, frequency, and purpose of any disclosure which may be made of such information, including the identification of the types of persons to whom the disclosure may be made. We may make your records available to employees, agents and contractors to install, market, provide, or audit cable service and to measure viewership and customer satisfaction on each occasion access is needed for the specific job at hand. Access for these purposes is routine, and does not occur with any specific frequency. We may also occasionally release our customer list to a consumer research organization to conduct market research for services provided and programs shown by the cable system. Access for these purposes occurs when needed and not with any specific frequency. Further, we make our customer list available each month to an independent billing house to send bills, to provide our customers information relating to their cable service or other services provided by us, and to provide our customers information relating to other products and services offered by third parties; to distributors each month for sending program guides; to programmers for marketing and promotions of their services carried on our system; to programmers and outside auditors to check our records whenever such audits are required, as needed; to attorneys and accountants on a continuous basis as necessary to render service to the company; to potential purchasers in connection with a system sale which occurs only at the time such sale is contemplated; to franchising authorities to demonstrate compliance with the franchise when requested; to mailing services as needed for system-related mailings to customers; and to collection services if required to collect past due bills at such time as bills are submitted for collection. Where utilized, customer information also is disclosed to our bill payment lock box service each month as necessary for processing customer payments.

Reader-unfriendly notice

Integrating Text and Visuals

Readers process information in different ways: visually by reading words, auditorially through hearing, kinesthetically by handling objects or doing tasks, and holistically through seeing how the whole relates to the parts. Traditional text has appealed to only one of those learning styles—the visual learner.

However, computers make it possible to integrate text and visuals, thus helping holistic learners process information more effectively.

> Computers have changed how paragraphs look. The modern "paragraph" may very well be a graphic with a caption that interprets the data.

Besides being sensitive to learning styles, good writers understand that some information is simply clearer if laid out in a graphic form. But interpreting the details with a complete caption—or strong topic sentence—is still important. The effective use of graphics draws the reader in to key points you wish to make. Often, when someone reads a memo you send, the only part that may receive attention will be a chart, graph, or graphic with a caption. Thus, effectively using these tools is critical.

Figure 4-3 shows how the same data has greater impact as a bar chart than as text. The text includes more historical explanation, but the visual "tells" the story more dramatically.

A. Text

The number of school districts continues to decline. In 1914, the state had 5,889 school districts—the largest number since statehood when schools were located within walking distance of every child. Between 1947 and 1965, almost 3,300 schools were annexed or consolidated. Incentives provided in 1990 fostered renewed interest in consolidation, reducing the number of school districts as of January 2002 to 543.

B. Visual

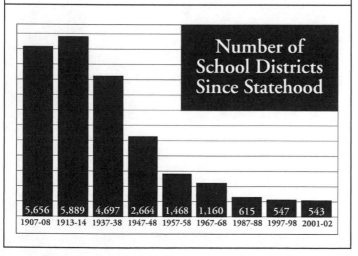

Number of School Districts Since Statehood

| 5,656 | 5,889 | 4,697 | 2,664 | 1,468 | 1,160 | 615 | 547 | 543 |
| 1907-08 | 1913-14 | 1937-38 | 1947-48 | 1957-58 | 1967-68 | 1987-88 | 1997-98 | 2001-02 |

Figure 4-3: Text versus visual impact
Source: Oklahoma State Department of Education, The Progress of Education Reform, Volume 7, *June 2002.*

ELEMENTS OF EXCELLENCE

Chapter 4 focused on how you can increase the effectiveness of your writing by developing strong paragraphs. This chapter explained the following points:

> The Ladder of Abstraction as a tool to guide your ability to convey your message to your reader through effective use of words.
> How to effectively craft paragraphs that state your key points and present information logically.
> The importance of integrating text information and visuals to assist the reader.

Chapter 5

Editing

Potential Problems	Strategies
Words that make reading difficult	Remember your audience by: • Eliminating or defining jargon for lay readers. • Preferring plain English. • Choosing an informal, personal style.
Complex or unclear words	Avoid pompous vocabulary and vague, abstract terms.
Wordiness, redundancy	Be concise and direct by: • Pruning wordy phrases. • Choosing action verbs. • Preferring active to passive verbs. • Eliminating hedgers and empty sentence beginnings.
Careless word choice	Choose words that say exactly what you mean. Always run spell-check. Then proofread.

Editing

< 89 >

Editing

< **90** >

Editing for Clear Style

Malcolm Forbes, founder and editor-in-chief of *Forbes Magazine*, offered this great advice: "*Be natural—write the way you talk.* Imagine [the reader] sitting in front of you—what would you say to him? . . . The acid test—read your letter out loud when you're done. You might get a shock—but you'll know for sure if it sounds natural." [*emphasis in the original*]

Too often, workplace writing lacks personality—it sounds like no *person* has written it and no *person* is addressed. In trying to sound professional, some writers mimic the same voice or tone—impersonal, complex, and harder to read than necessary. In editing, you begin the re-visioning—or looking again at what you've written—that allows you to change a reader-unfriendly style into a plain style that has a "voice." To begin rewriting for an effective voice, ask, "Is my style precise, appropriate, clear, and concise?"

> Say all you have to say in the fewest possible words, or your reader will be sure to skip them; and in the plainest possible words or he will certainly misunderstand them.
>
> JOHN RUSKIN

PITFALLS

Write like you talk—but only if your talk is right.

There is definite wisdom in the idea of writing like you speak, as it connects you to other people and makes the writer–reader transaction more natural. When I say "right" talk, I am referring to proper and professional writing. There is a place for slang and opinion in almost every piece of modern professional writing, but be sure not to take it beyond what is professional. It is in your best interest to have someone proofread your writing if you think you are being a bit risqué.

Always avoid:

> Profanity.
> Racial stereotypes or slang.
> Sexist language.
> "In-speak"—phrases that you and a select few understand, but many do not.

Precise

Choose words that say what you mean.

Not: The Information Services manager who said, "Our goal is to create a huge data suppository."

Choose words with precise, vivid connotations.

Interest rates *ballooned* for two reasons. To further *cement* their existing relationship . . .

Appropriate

Replace high-sounding words with plain English.

He advised . . .
He indicated . . . } He said . . .
He notified . . .

Use *you* and *I.*

This writer has been notified by your office that . . . ➤ As you told me . . .

Clear

Beware of vague, abstract words.

The tank is almost full. ➤ The tank contains 14 gallons, with a 16-gallon capacity.

Use pronouns that clearly refer to a noun.

This proves the breakdown occurred because . . . ➤ This series of events proves the breakdown occurred because . . .

Concise

Cross out redundant phrases.

In the amount of $10.00 ➤ $10.00

Never use several words when one word will do.

With respect to ➤ about
In conjunction with ➤ with
In order to ➤ to

Resurrect strong verbs from derived nouns and adjectives.

Consideration ➤ consider
Decision ➤ decide
Accomplishment ➤ accomplish
Beneficial for ➤ benefits

Replace passive verbs by using the "Who does what" sentence pattern.

The decision was made by us. ➤ We decided . . .

Omit empty sentence beginnings such as "There" and "It."

There is overwhelming evidence that suggests . . . ➤ Overwhelming evidence suggests . . .

Polishing for Precision

Choose the words that say precisely what you intend.
Words carry two types of meaning:

1. **Denotation**, which is the literal or generally accepted meaning
2. **Connotation**, or the implied or associated meanings

For example, *leave* means "to exit" or "go away from." So does *abandon,* but the latter implies an emergency (the connotation). With both words you would no longer inhabit the same space (the denotation); however, if you "abandon," you leave quickly, not intending to return.

To choose the precise word, edit for the following:

> **Exact connotations**—Choose words that carry the precise meaning you intend. Gain as much mileage from your words as you can. For example, do you mean "meet" or "gather" or "confer"? Is it a "conference" or an "event" or a "symposium" or a "presentation"?

> **Fresh vocabulary**—Choose interesting words. We tend to rely on the same overused vocabulary of about 600 words. Dust off your larger working vocabulary. Instead of *provide,* try *give* or *send* or *offer* or *mail* or *ship* or *explain* or . . .

> **Unanticipated meaning**—Do *not* use unfamiliar words you discover in the thesaurus. If a word is not part of your working vocabulary, do not use it. It will sound unnatural, plus you can make an embarrassing error. One banking memo that analyzed a new federal banking regulation began, "This is to explain the prophylactic regulation." Right meaning; wrong connotation.

In interviewing Ernest Hemingway, a reporter said he had heard Hemingway had a hard time with a chapter of *For Whom the Bell Tolls*. Hemingway said that, yes, it required revising. The reporter asked how many revisions, and Hemingway answered, "37." Asked what the problem was, Papa replied, "Getting the words right."

Most workplace writers do not have that kind of time to master just the right word. But they should choose their words wisely to gain clarity and impact.

Determining Appropriateness

Traditional writing valued one style—the formal. Complex vocabulary, elaborate sentences, and strict rules marked the educated person. But such complexity assumed that readers had the time and inclination to enjoy text, savoring the development of arguments and learned vocabulary. Some still do. But most modern workplace readers prefer a more direct, clear style to ornate complexity.

Thus, one style does not fit all documents. In editing, you need to decide which words will be appropriate for this audience on this occasion. Some documents will be formal; others should be informal. Some will omit personal references; others will focus on "you"—the reader, customer, coworker. Therefore, edit your text to meet the needs of your different readers by observing the following guidelines.

Be Sensitive to Jargon

Walter Kaufmann elaborated on the social implications of proliferating jargon: "Men love jargon. It is so palpable, tangible, visible, audible; it makes so obvious what one has learned; it satisfies the craving for results. It is impressive for the uninitiated. It makes one feel that one belongs. Jargon divides men into Us and Them."

Jargon is the shared vocabulary of any group—a profession, a company, a social club, a family. Who determines the fine line between a precise, professional vocabulary (appropriate jargon) and meaningless verbiage? Your readers. For experts (or members of the group), jargon expresses complex ideas clearly and concisely. However, jargon excludes nonexperts. When used with the wrong audience, it confuses and divides. You will use jargon in the workplace. However, be careful.

Of course, we have no trouble recognizing someone else's jargon. We've all trudged through an incoherent insurance policy or legal document. The trend, however, is away from using jargon. These days, the professions, insurance companies, and government are rewriting documents in a readable style to be more customer-friendly—and clear.

Workplace Application—Promissory Note

Old: "No extension of time for payment, or delay in enforcement hereof, nor any renewal of this note, with or without notice, shall operate as a waiver of any rights hereunder or release the obligation of any maker, guarantor, endorser, or any other accommodation party."

New: "We can delay enforcing any of our rights without losing them."

Jargon

Purpose: The following exercise will test your ability to remove jargon from statements that are unclear. These statements were supposed to communicate professionally. See if you can translate each into plain English.

1. Witnesseth: That parties to these presents, each in consideration of the undertakings, promises and agreements on the part of the other herein contained, have undertaken, promised, and agreed and do hereby undertake, promise and agree, each for itself, its successors and assigns, as follows:

2. A bulletin sent to parents described a new Houston education program:

   "Our school's cross-graded, multi-ethnic, individualized learning program is designed to enhance the concept of an open-ended learning program with emphasis on a continuum of multi-ethnic, academically enriched learning, using the identified intellectually gifted child as the agent or director of his own learning. Major emphasis is on cross-graded, multi-ethnic learning with the main objective being to learn respect for the uniqueness of a person."

   (One parent responded to this bulletin: "Dear Principal: I have a college degree, speak two foreign languages, and know four Indian dialects. I've attended a number of county fairs and three goat ropings but I haven't the faintest idea as to what the hell you are talking about.")

3. From an address on economic and financial management:

   "A slow-up of the slowdown is not as good as an upturn of the downcurve, but it is better than either a speedup of the slowdown or a deepening of the downcurve—and it suggests the climate is right for an adjustment of the readjustment.

   "Turning to unemployment, we find a definite decrease in the rate of increase—which shows there is a letting up of the letdown. If the slowdown should speed up, the decrease in the rate of increase of unemployment would turn into an increase in the rate of decrease of unemployment.

"We expect a leveling-off—referred to on Wall Street as bumping along rock bottom—sometime this winter. This will be followed by a gentle pickup, then a faster pickup, a slow-down of the pickup, and finally a leveling off in the spring."

4. He was proceeding to install pedestrian heads on mast arm poles at the southwest corner.

5. As lit capacity is eliminated from the market and the long-haul carriers bring their guns to bear on the metro marketplace, which will provide on-ramps to their high capacity cores, we predict an uptick in the competitive telecom marketplace will unfold. ▪

Analysis. How did you react to this jargon? What did you think as you read the statements? How would (or did) you respond? It is easy to criticize other people's jargon, but we are comfortable with our own. Others react to our jargon just as we did to the preceding statements. (See Figure 5-1.)

Figure 5-1: Writing to impress versus to express. *Source*: Cartoon by Jeff MacNelly. Courtesy of Tribune Media Services, Inc. All rights reserved. Reprinted with permission.

Prefer the Plain Style

Although not exactly jargon, an inflated vocabulary of "businessese" has become a specialized language of its own. Generally, this style is too formal and wordy. Growing out of a Latinate vocabulary, it produces an overblown voice that can easily be pared to more concise, clear statements. The plain style, on the other hand, is clearer and easier to read. It is also appropriate.

> It's been a long time since I've heard someone say, 'I can't understand what he's saying; he must be highly intelligent.'
>
> DOUGLAS MUELLER

TIPS

There is nothing wrong with big words. In fact, a rich vocabulary helps you find the word with the precise meaning you need. However, choose the familiar term instead of the formal *if* the two do not differ in meaning (see Table 5-1).

TABLE 5-1. Choose the Familiar Form	
Formal	Familiar
apprise	mention
ascertain	determine, find out
avail oneself	use
cognizant of	aware of, recognize
commence	begin
contingent upon	depend on
deem	think
discontinue	stop
endeavor	try
enhance	improve
facilitate	help, ease
finalize	complete
forward	send
generate	create
indicate	say, suggest

(continued)

Editing

TABLE 5-1. *(continued)*	
Formal	Familiar
initiate	start, begin
interface	meet
per	as, by, according to
presently	now
prior to	before
provide	send, give, offer
render	make, give
subsequent to	after
transmit	send, give
transpire	happen
utilize	use

YOUR TURN

Formal Style

Purpose: Following are a number of practice exercises that will test your ability to edit. In plain English, what were the writers of the following statements talking about?

1. The troop leader told his men that "the movement to the new station will be implemented by means of wheeled, gas-operated vehicles."

Solution: The troops will move to the new station in trucks.

2. Illumination is required to be extinguished on these premises.

Solution: Turn out the lights.

3. This construction will encourage the use of leg power for vertical pedestrian circulation.

Solution: The shopping mall will use staircases.

4. Packing is always an issue, whether in the air or ground, you must have enough for your expedition to accommodate your necessities.

Solution: Packing is a problem because you need the essentials when you travel.

5. If you should have any questions or comments, please feel free to contact myself at your convenience. Once again thanks for your cooperation and support. It has been a pleasure dealing with your organization and our relationship shall continue to strengthen.

Solution: Please call if you have questions. We appreciate your continued cooperation and look forward to strengthening our relationship. ■

YOUR TURN

Editing for an Inflated Style

Translate the inflated letter that follows into plain English.

> Dear David:
>
> Enclosed please find the above referenced written Consent for your execution. It is required that we request your signature, your obtainment of the signature of Patterson O. Smithfield, and the subsequent restoration of the original document to myself. I will then be responsible for the transmission of this Consent to the remainder of the Board of Directors for their respective approbations.

Editing for inflated style

Use a You Focus

A "you focus" increases the readability of a document by pulling your reader into the conversation. That means that you speak directly to the reader, preferring "you" to "I" or "we." In writing a draft, we tend to focus on "I": what I did and what I want. In editing, refocus the text on your reader, "you."

Improving the You Focus

Purpose: Revise the following letter to improve its you attitude. Instead of focusing on what "I need," emphasize what you [the customer] can do to achieve the results *you* want. Your revisions will also improve the letter's customer focus.

July 30, 200__

Walter Lee
5489 River Lane
City, ST 78957

Mr. Lee,

In order to add Jamie to your account I need you both to please sign the enclosed signature card. I need you to sign in three places, once on the front by your name and twice on the back by the highlighted X's. Then I just need Jamie's signature one time on the front of the card by the highlighted X. I have also provided a postage-paid envelope for you to return the signature card at your earliest convenience.

If you have any questions or concerns please feel free to call. I have included my business card with the branch number. Thank you.

Sincerely,

Customer Service Representative

Improving the you focus

Prefer Positive to Negative

Studies show that readers process positive statements more quickly and accurately than they do identical information stated negatively. A positive statement is also more compelling. Therefore, you should replace negative phrases with positive phrases, if you can. For example:

Negative	**Positive**
Please do not hesitate to call.	Please call.
If you cannot find the information before Monday, it won't matter.	Waiting to find the information on Monday would be fine.

Workplace Application—Negative

The following disclaimer appears on a law firm's Web site, the purpose of which, presumably, is to attract clients. Legally the firm must state that the Web site does not contain legal advice or constitute an agreement to represent a client. However, the negative language could certainly block a potential client's interest.

Disclaimer

The material on this Web site is provided for informational purposes, and neither Law nor its attorneys make any guarantee that the material is kept up to date or is correct or complete. . . . No attorney of Law will represent a client in any jurisdiction in which that attorney is not licensed to practice law. . . .

The information presented is NOT intended as a substitute for specific legal advice or opinions, and the transmission of this information is NOT intended to create an attorney-client relationship between sender and receiver. . . .

While we would like to hear from you, we cannot represent you until we know that doing so will not create a conflict of interest. Please do not send us any information about any matter. . . .

In the event that this communication is not in conformity with the regulations of any state, this law firm is not willing to accept representation based on this communication.

Negative tone

Based on this disclaimer, it sounds as if the firm can't do much and doesn't want new clients. Compare that negative tone to the following reworded disclaimer that accomplishes the same goal—legal protection for another firm—with a more positive tone.

Workplace Application—Positive

> Please contact any of our attorneys or call one of our four offices to initiate possible representation by Legal Partners. A standard conflict-of-interest procedure will be followed to ensure the integrity of client interests, with follow-up made by the attorney whose expertise is best suited for counsel in your matter.
>
> Legal Partners publishes this and other business communications for informational purposes only. This communication does NOT substitute for specific legal advice or opinions. Further, the publication of this information is NOT intended to create an attorney-client relationship.

Positive tone

Choose Unbiased Language

Avoiding stereotyping through word choice is a relatively recent communication concern. As the ideas of traditionally male and female occupations have changed, our sense of appropriate language use has also changed. Why distract a reader from your message through a poor word choice? The following guidelines suggest graceful ways to avoid sexual reference without cluttering your writing with awkward "he/she," "gentleperson," and "humankind" alternatives.

Avoid "man-words" when referring to all people.

Instead of	Use
mankind	humanity, people
If a man completes the job . . .	If a person completes the job . . .
man-made	synthetic, manufactured
manpower	workers, workforce
businessman	executive, manager, owner
congressman	member of Congress
salesman	salesperson, clerk
fireman, policeman	firefighter, police officer
chairman	chair, chairperson

Use nonsexist pronouns.

> Choose gender-neutral words when referring to all people.

The average man drives *The average person drives a car . . .*
his car . . .

> Use the plural form.

The average person drives *Most people drive their cars . . .*
his car . . .

> Use a neutral pronoun.

When a consumer looks for *When looking for a bargain, one may*
a bargain, he may buy . . . *buy . . . or . . . you may buy . . .*
          or . . . he or she may buy . . .

> Use a passive rather than an active verb.

Every employee participates *Every employee participates in the*
in the health plan. He should *healthplan. The forms may may*
pick up the forms . . .   *be picked up . . .*

Avoid sexual stereotyping in addressing correspondence.

> Use the reader's name whenever possible:

Dear Mr. Smith:
Dear Ms. Wong:

The courtesy title Ms. is now widely accepted and solves the irrelevant question of a woman's marital status.

> Use a neutral term when the sex of the reader is unknown:

Dear Executive:
Dear Manager:

> Begin the letter without a salutation:

Simpson Hams, Inc.
105 Main Street
Sussex, Virginia 10007

Please send me a catalogue and price list for your products . . .

Increasing Clarity

Choose Specific and Concrete Words

Remember that words lower on the Ladder of Abstraction are clearer (see Chapter 4). For example, "Vigorous physical exercise at an early time is an excellent way to start the day" can be made more specific by saying, "Fifty pushups before breakfast can start the day right."

YOUR TURN

Clarity

Purpose: Rewrite each of the following sentences so that it expresses the same idea in specific rather than abstract terms.

1. The cost of the equipment is too high.

_____

2. The stock market is off.

_____

3. What he needs is some kind of disciplinary treatment.

_____

4. They had no one good way of doing things, and it took a lot of time getting things done.

_____

_____

Editing

Check for Clear Pronoun Reference

Pronouns take the place of nouns. Two pronouns—*this* and *which*—are often used carelessly to refer to an entire idea rather than to a particular noun. You can easily correct this "broad reference" by inserting a noun. For example,

Vague: The materials are scheduled to arrive next week. *This* will enable us to start production immediately.

Clearer: The materials are scheduled to arrive next week. *Their arrival* will enable us to start production immediately.

Vague: We expect to receive several requests, *which* should take awhile to complete.

Clearer: We expect to receive several requests, *a process which* should take awhile to complete.

Clear Pronoun Reference

Purpose: First, circle every "this" in the following paragraph and see whether you can tie each one clearly to the noun it refers to. If not, edit the sentence to make the reference clear, either by changing the text or inserting the missing noun after "this."

Implementing vendor specific validations will decrease error/rejection rates, necessitating fewer supplements and less provisioning/vendor communications. This will decrease both order cost and order time. As this is an intensive process, requiring thorough requirements analysis for each specific vendor, this will only be implemented for our major trading partners, the eight regional suppliers. This will also allow us greater applicability of our service agreements, as these are valid only for clean (error-free) orders. ■

Conserving Words

Another mark of the too-formal style is wordiness. Replacing deadwood phrases and choosing strong action verbs will improve the clarity and power of your sentences. Look for the following "red flag" phrases to remove 20 to 30 percent—sometimes 50 percent—of the words, without loss of content.

Prune the Deadwood

Eliminate words that take up space without adding any meaning. They are like deadwood in shrubs—cluttering the plant without contributing substance.

Instead of	Use
Redundancies—phrases that repeat meaning	
in the amount of $10.59	$10.59
during the period of June 1 through July 15	from June 1 through June 15
located in **the state of** Texas	in Texas
red **in color**	red
the reason is because	because
Filler words—words that add no meaning	
in **the area of** Accounting	in Accounting
in **the field of** engineering	in engineering
on a daily **basis**	daily
with an efficient **manner**	efficiently
Preposition + noun + preposition —clumps of prepositional phrases that can be replaced with one word	
in order to	to
due to the fact that	because
in the event of	if
in regard to	about
in conjunction with	with
at the present time	now
at this point in time	now

Examples of Pruning Deadwood

~~In an effort~~ to clarify our records, ~~we ask that you~~ provide additional information concerning your ownership.   *please*

To clarify our records, please provide additional information concerning your ownership.

For ~~the purpose of~~ this report, the current compliance status is ~~the status~~ for ~~the six month period~~ October 1, 2003, through March 31, 2004.

For this report, the current compliance status is for October 1, 2003, through March 31, 2004.

Until ~~such time as~~ the necessary corrective documents are prepared ~~in order~~ ~~for~~ *so* the interest *can* ~~to~~ be owned equally as intended, I have placed the interest of Sara Smith in suspense and will continue to pay Sam Smith ~~individually~~ and Tom Smith individually.

Until the necessary corrective documents are prepared so the interest can be owned equally as intended, I have placed the interest of Sara Smith in suspense and will continue to pay Sam Smith and Tom Smith individually.

> I want to get rid of the 'chatter' in my writing.
>
> AN ADMINISTRATIVE ASSISTANT

Strengthen Your Verbs

The power of the English language is in the verbs. Tap that power by replacing weak verbs, nouns, and adjectives with strong action verbs. Some examples include:

Instead of	Use
Nouns formed from verbs— verbs frequently ending in *-tion, -sion, -son, -ment, -ance,* or *-ence.*	***Strong action***
make a recommendation	recommend
make an investigation	investigate
make a comparison of	compare
make a decision to	decide

> Author Jimmy Breslin, describing his anxiety about impending brain surgery: "If anything happens to my verbs, I'll be on home relief."

Editing

Instead of	Use
be in agreement with	agree
have a preference for	prefer
be in compliance with	comply
"to be" verb forms—sometimes paired with adjectives that hide a strong verb.	***Strong action verbs***
is beneficial to	benefits
is persuasive	persuades
is agreeable to	agrees
Passive voice—verbs in which the object is being acted on (see "Prefer Active to Passive Verbs")	***Active voice***—Who does what?
A decision was made by the committee . . .	The committee decided . . .
The program is used to monitor . . .	The program monitors . . .
The form should be sent to . . .	Send the form to . . .
Empty openings—*there* and *it*	***Substance up front***
It is necessary that we begin to . . .	We must begin to . . .
There were thousands of spectators cheering . . .	Thousands of spectators cheered . . .
It is the recommendation of the committee that . . .	The committee recommends . . .
There were several suggestions made during the meeting . . .	Several suggestions were made . . .
Hedgers—phrases that limit responsibility	***Take a stand***
I think that the data shows . . .	The data shows . . .
It is my opinion that we should change vendors . . .	We should change vendors . . .

Workplace Application—Conciseness

Notice the difference in clarity and conciseness between the original and the revised versions of the letter to Chairman Jones that follow.

RE: Revised Letter to Chairman Jones on FERC Administrative Procedures

Attached for your review is a redraft of the December 20 letter initially intended to be sent to FERC Chairman Jones by Seaway's Jim Thompson regarding FERC administrative problems. It now incorporates the comments you provided as well as those of the other committee members. I hope you will take the opportunity to review the attached draft one more time and submit your comments to me. While there is no deadline set by our committee for a response, if you could supply something within the next two weeks, I would be most appreciative.

As you will recall the letter details problems, including the processing of orders by the Commission and the position taken by staff in rate cases and settlements, and offers solutions. Initially it was to serve as the basis for a meeting between Thompson and Jones. However, APP Director Kimberly Mason was made aware of the existence of this letter and, due to her interest in the matter, our final work product will be sent to her.

Attachment

Original memo—169 words

RE: Revised Letter to Chairman Jones on FERC Administrative Procedures

Please review and submit your comments within the next two weeks on the attached redraft of the December 20 letter from Seaway's Jim Thompson, Chairman of the Regulatory Affairs Committee, to FERC Chairman Jones. Incorporated are your comments and those of other committee members regarding the FERC administrative problems, including processing of orders by the Commission and the position taken by staff in rate cases and settlements.

This letter was to serve as the basis for a meeting between Thompson and Jones, but Kimberly Mason, APP Director, has shown an interest in this letter and our final work product will be sent to her.

Attachment

Revised version—104 words

Prefer Active to Passive Verbs

Passive verbs produce three unwanted results by:

1. Adding unnecessary words.
2. Robbing sentences of the force of *someone-doing-something*.
3. Masking responsibility if the actor is omitted.

To make your sentences more effective and more concise, you should prefer active to passive verbs.

Active: George planned the retreat.

Passive: The retreat was planned by George.

The passive consists of this construction:

to be [*is, was, were, been, being*]   + a verb ending in -*ed,* -*en,* or -*t*
                         ↑   [loved, seen, hit]
           auxiliary verb   +   **past participle**

plus a stated or implied "by" *prepositional phrase*

Passive to Active

Purpose: Rewrite these passive sentences so that they have active verbs.

1. Checks presented for payment must be approved by GNMA.

_____

_____

2. A training manual or handout is provided for each participant.

_____

_____

3. The analyst is required to make determinations of the sample volume for initial use.

_____

_____

4. It was determined there was a need to educate and inform our employees about industry issues.

_____

_____

Editing

Editing for Strong Verbs

Purpose: Edit these sentences to strengthen the verbs and increase the balance between active and passive.

1. The age range of children admitted to the Shelter is from birth to 17.

_____

_____

2. This was an occurrence that was unforeseen by the company and was outside of their control.

_____

_____

3. There are some overall concepts that represent a different approach than the current system.

_____

_____

4. In order to allow for an adequate evaluation, a sufficient amount of time is required.

_____

_____

5. Upon clicking on the icon with your remote, a second page with detailed information is displayed.

_____

_____

Editing

Editing

Purpose: These sentences are clogged with deadwood and weak verbs. Eliminate the "chatter."

1. We are in receipt of a fifty dollar, $50., money order payable to General Utility Company.

_____

_____

2. My situation is that I have a request from Express Service for this service.

_____

_____

3. If there were any way to consolidate these accounts, month-end reconcilement would be greatly simplified.

_____

_____

4. I do feel that we need to continue the verification process that currently exists to ensure we are delivering an accurate instrument back to the field locations.

_____

_____

5. The survey was targeted at people who live in Austin, Texas, and information was gathered about their shopping habits.

_____

_____

More Practice Editing

Purpose: The following paragraph is typical old-style, inflated text, laden with complex vocabulary, jargon, and wordy phrases. Revise it for clarity and conciseness:

> Over the past few months, it has come to our attention that several of the district locations do not currently utilize these statements. Our understanding is that there are alternative sources of the same information (e.g., the Cumulative file) that many locations access through various computer extractions. Apparently, these extractions are providing the various locations with cost information sufficient to meet their needs. Accordingly, for the purpose of determining if issuance of the statements can be discontinued, we are asking that you review the usefulness of our Detail Cost statements to the Production Department. Removal of the requirements for issuance of such statements might possibly result in elimination of what appears to be a duplication of efforts on the part of our Department. [123 words]

Checking for Word Demons

Finally, check your spelling and word usage. Errors distract readers from your content and suggest that you are careless. Beware of words that sound alike or are easily confused. You want to avoid the embarrassment of the manager whose proposal to move his department ended with, "The move will certainly increase the moral of the department." Also, be sure your dictionary is current. Language evolves as new words enter or old guidelines change. Using words correctly proves you are careful with your written product.

Some of these word demons include:

accent, ascent, assent. *Accent* implies speech emphasis or pronunciation. *Ascent* is "to climb," whereas *assent* means "to agree."

accept, except. *Accept* is a verb meaning "to agree to." Example: We *accept* your offer. *Except* involves leaving something out. Example: Everyone went *except* Joan.

access, excess. *Access* means "approaching" or "entering," whereas *excess* implies "more than enough" or "too much" of something. Examples: He gained *access* to the vault. He found an *excess* of old stock certificates.

advice, advise. *Advice* is a noun that means "giving one's opinion." Example: Here is my *advice*. *Advise* is the verb. Example: I *advise* you not to go. *Advise* has the –z sound.

affect, effect. *Affect* is a verb except in some professional jargon. Example: The change *affected* her attitude. *Effect* is usually a noun. Example: The *effect* of the change was dramatic. However, *effect* is sometimes used as a verb meaning "to create" or "produce." The good news *effected* great joy in Mudville.

allusion, illusion. *Allusion* is "an indirect reference to," whereas *illusion* is a "false vision." Examples: Her *allusion* to Homer suggested that the mythological gods were an *illusion*.

a lot, alot, allot. *A lot,* meaning "quite a bit," is always spelled with two words (not *alot*). Example: She had *a lot* of talent. *Allot* means "to set aside" or "apportion." He took his *allotted* share.

already, all ready. *Already* means "by this time." Example: The car had *already* passed the corner. *All ready* means "totally ready." Example: We are *all ready* to go.

amount, number. *Amount* is used with a bulk item. Example: She had a large *amount* of time on her hands. *Number* is used with countable items. Example: She had a *number* of days available.

and etc. Redundant. *Etc.* means "and others."

angel, angle. *Angel* is a heavenly being, whereas *angle* is where two lines come together.

anxious, eager. *Anxious* comes from the root word *anxiety*. It implies worry. Example: He was *anxious* about her well-being. *Eager* means "looking forward to." Example: She was *eager* to get to work.

anyone, any one. *Anyone* is an indefinite pronoun. Example: Does *anyone* know when the meeting is? *Any one* refers to a particular one person or thing. Example: You can choose *any one* of the items in the drawing.

appraise, apprise. *Appraise* is an estimation of value. Example: The agent *appraised* the property too low. *Apprise* means "to tell." I will *apprise* you when the check arrives.

bad, badly. *Bad* is an adjective, the opposite of *good*. Example: He had a *bad* cold. *Badly* is the adverb. Example: He limped *badly* after the accident.

bare, bear. *Bare* is an adjective meaning "nude." *Bear* is either a large animal or a verb meaning "to carry." One new female employee got quite a response when she e-mailed her coworkers: "I have several questions and announcements about the library, so please *bare* with me."

between, among. Use *between* when referring to two persons or things and *among* when referring to more than two. Examples: Nothing should come *between* you and me, but there may be problems *among* all the candidates.

breath, breathe. *Breath* is the noun, and *breathe* is the verb. Examples: She took a *breath* of fresh air and then continued to *breathe* normally.

can, may. Traditionally, *can* meant "to be able to," and *may* meant "to have permission to." Examples: I *can* send you the report tomorrow. *May* I call to see that it arrived?

capital, capitol. *Capital* refers to the city which is the seat of government and to wealth. *Capitol* means the building where the legislature meets. Examples: We drove to the *capital* and had no trouble finding the *capitol* building. The plan is to raise *capital* for the highway project.

cite, site, sight. *Cite* means "to refer to." Example: He *cited* several sources. *Site* is a place. Example: The *site* of the new library has been chosen. *Sight* is what our eyes give us. Example: You are a *sight* for sore eyes.

clothes, cloths. People wear *clothes* and use *cloths* to wipe their faces.

coarse, course. *Coarse* is an adjective meaning "rough feeling." Example: Sandpaper is *coarse*. *Course* is a noun that means "a way of going."

Example: I took a *course* in speech so that I could follow a new *course* in the company.

compliment, complement. Both are used as nouns and verbs. *Compliment* means "to say something nice," and it also refers to what is said. Examples: He *complimented* her on her good report. She appreciated the *compliment*. *Complement* means "to complete." Examples: The analysis will *complement* the last report. The wine was a nice *complement* to the meal.

conscience, conscious. *Conscience* is having a sense of right and wrong; *conscious* means "being aware." Examples: His *conscience* made him *conscious* of his extreme error in judgment.

contractions. In informal business documents, using contractions, such as *we're, you're,* and *it's,* is acceptable. Do not use them in formal reports, proposals, or minutes.

council, counsel. A *council* is a legislative body. *Counsel* as a verb means "to give advice"; as a noun it is the advice itself or an attorney.

decent, descend, dissent. *Decent,* derived from *decency,* means "proper." *Descend* means "to go down." *Dissent* means "to disagree" (verb) or "difference of opinion"(noun).

device, devise. *Device* is the noun meaning "an object used." Example: She took the *device* away from the inept worker. *Devise* [-z sound] is a verb meaning to plan. Example: We *devised* a new strategy to increase sales.

disinterested, uninterested. *Disinterested* means "impartial," whereas *uninterested* means "not interested." Examples: I hope to find a *disinterested,* not an *uninterested,* judge for the contest.

effect, affect. See *affect, effect.*

e.g., i.e. Both are Latin abbreviations for transitions and are followed by a comma. *e.g.* means "for example." Example: We planned several United Way events, *e.g.,* a drawing and a rally. *i.e.* specifies "that is." Example: He will arrive when he can, *i.e.,* at noon.

elicit, illicit. *Elicit* is a verb meaning "to draw out." Example: He tried to *elicit* the information from the suspect. *Illicit* is an adjective meaning "illegal." Example: The *illicit* activity finally came to light.

eminent, imminent. *Eminent* means "outstanding," whereas *imminent* means "occurring very soon." Examples: The arrival of our *eminent* speaker is *imminent.*

except, accept. See *accept, except.*

everyday, every day. *Everyday* is an adjective meaning "ordinary." Example: The *everyday* event had become boring. *Every day* means "each day." Example: We had the boring event *every day.*

farther, further. *Farther* involves distance. Example: He could drive *farther* than anyone in a day. *Further* implies greater amount or degree. Example: She was *further* along with the project than anyone expected.

fewer, less. Like *number* and *amount, fewer* and *less* distinguish countable from indivisible items. Examples: Because our department had *fewer* sales this month [countable], we expect *less* profit [indivisible].

good, well. *Good* is an adjective describing a positive condition. Example: Here is a commendation for your *good* presentation. *Well* is usually an adverb describing how something occurred. Example: You did *well* in your presentation.

immigrate, emigrate. *Immigrate* means "to move into a country," whereas *emigrate* means "to permanently move from one place to another." Examples: The scientist plans to *emigrate* from the Far East and then *immigrate* to the United States.

imply, infer. The speaker *implies;* the listener *infers.* Examples: He *implied* that he would recommend our group. I *inferred* from what he said that he was pleased with our work.

in, into. *In* suggests a location. Example: Put the file *in* the drawer. *Into* implies a movement or change. Example: The assistant settled *into* her new position easily.

innocence, innocents. *Innocence* is a condition of blamelessness. *Innocents* are the people who are blameless.

insure, ensure, assure. Traditional usage distinguished between *insure,* meaning "to obtain financial protection," from *ensure,* meaning "to make certain." Current dictionaries now also accept "make certain" as a secondary definition for *insure. Assure* means "to promise." Examples: I will *ensure* that he mails the check to *insure* the new car. Can you *assure* me that he has insurance?

its, it's. *Its* is the possessive pronoun. Example: The department always schedules *its* meetings early. *It's* is the contraction meaning "it is." If a pronoun has an apostrophe, it **must** be a contraction (*they're, you're, it's*). No possessive pronoun takes an apostrophe (*his, hers, ours, its*).

lie, lay. *Lie* is an intransitive verb, meaning that it is a complete action in itself and takes no object. Example: I am going to *lie* down. *Lay* is transitive; the action carries through to an object. Example: I will *lay* the report on your desk.

loose, lose. *Loose* is an adjective meaning "not tight." Example: The gem was *loose* in its setting. *Lose* [-z sound] is a verb meaning "to not win or to misplace." Example: The candidate hated to *lose* the election.

may. See *can, may.*

maybe, may be. *Maybe* is an adverb meaning "perhaps." Example: *Maybe* we will go. *May be* is a verb form suggesting a conditional state of being. Example: The report *may be* on her desk.

moral, morale. *Moral* (mōr'-el) is an adjective describing a social judgment. Example: His actions were always *moral*. *Morale* (mo-răl') is a noun that means "mental or emotional condition." Example: Department *morale* was low during the layoffs.

myself. *Myself* is a reflexive or intensive pronoun (like *himself, herself, ourselves*) and requires a double. The doer and the receiver must be the same person. Example: I hit *myself* on the thumb. Do not use it alone. Example [**wrong**]: The client will call George or *myself* when she is ready.

number. See *amount, number.*

passed, past. *Passed* is past tense of *pass*. Example: He *passed* the test. *Past* is a noun or adjective describing former time. Example: In the *past,* we always received our order on time.

patience, patients. *Patience* is a human quality of endurance. *Patients* are sick people.

per. Overly formal business jargon used to replace *pursuant to, per* can also mean "according to" or "by means of." Limiting its use to the accurate mathematical usage [fee *per* hour] improves clarity.

percent, percentage. *Percent* (spelled as one word) means one part of a hundred. Example: The election drew only 46 *percent* of eligible voters. *Percentage* means a proportion or share of a total. Example: That *percentage* is terrible.

persecuted, prosecuted. *Persecuted* means "to harass or oppress;" *prosecute* means "to bring to trial." The Israeli government *prosecuted* former Nazi guards who had *persecuted* the inmates.

personnel, personal. *Personnel* (pûr' se-nêl') is a noun meaning "the people in an organization." Example: Our *personnel* are excellent salespersons. *Personal* (pûr' se-nel) is an adjective meaning "private." Example: This is a *personal* message.

phrasal words such as *sign up, shut in, break down,* and *follow up.* These informal words are **usually** spelled as two words when they show action (verbs), hyphenated when they describe (adjectives), and closed up as one word when they name (nouns). Check a current dictionary or style manual to be sure. Examples:

> We will *break down* the display after the show. Here is the *break-down* plan. I almost had a *breakdown,* it was so much work.

> I will *follow up* next week. Do you have the *follow-up* list?
> [exception] I will call you about your *follow-up.*

precede, proceed. *Precede* means "to go before." Example: I will *precede* you in the processional. Remember that *pre-* means "before." *Proceed* means "to go forward." He will *proceed* to raise the tough questions during the meeting.

principal, principle. *Principal* is "the head of" or "most important." Example: The school *principal* is head of staff. *Principle* is a basic rule. Example: The *principal* reason for my objections rested on our strong *principle* regarding honesty.

quiet, quit, quite. *Quiet* is an adjective meaning "without sound." *Quit* is a verb meaning "to stop." *Quite* is an intensifier meaning "very." Examples: I do not want to *quit* the club because the *quiet* atmosphere is *quite* soothing.

real, really. *Real* is an adjective meaning "authentic." *Really* is an adverb. Examples: We *really* need to work to achieve *real* success.

rise, raise. *Rise* is an intransitive verb, meaning that it is a complete action in itself and takes no object. Example: The sun *rises* in the morning. *Raise* is transitive; the action carries through to an object. Example: I will *raise* the window shade if it's too dark in here.

shall, will. American usage accepts *will* for the future tense of all verbs; *shall* is reserved for formal requests or to show determination. Examples: We *will* go with you to the conference. We *shall* overcome.

sit, set. *Sit* is an intransitive verb, meaning that it is a complete action in itself and takes no object. Example: I am going to *sit* down. *Set* is transitive; the action carries through to an object. Example: I will *set* the report on your desk.

stationary, stationery. *Stationary* is an adjective meaning "unmovable." Example: The *stationary* equipment was rusted. *Stationery* is a noun meaning "paper." I bought new *stationery* for the sales letters.

their, they're, there. *Their* is the possessive pronoun. Example: They asked *their* heir to come visit them. *They're* is a contraction for *they are*. Example: *They're* planning to attend. *There* is an adverb, the opposite of *here*. Example: Put the lamp *there* on the desk.

then, than. *Then* is an adverb identifying time. Example: *Then* they left for the airport. *Than* is a conjunction that involves a comparison. Example: Our competition is more aggressive *than* we are.

thorough, through, though. *Thorough* is an adjective meaning "complete." Example: She performed a *thorough* audit. *Through* is a preposition or adverb meaning "among" or "complete." Examples: When she was *through,* she went *through* all her records. *Though* is a conjunction similar to *although*. Example: We won, even *though* he tripped at the finish line.

to, too, two. *To* is a preposition of direction. Example: I sent the letter *to* the correct address. *Too* means "also." Example: Did you send a letter *too*? *Two* is the number 2.

unique. Meaning one of a kind, *unique* does not take qualifiers. Something is *unique,* **not** very unique.

uninterested, disinterested. See *disinterested, uninterested.*

> The only stupid thing about words is the spelling of them.
>
> LAURA INGALLS WILDER

weather, whether. *Weather* is a noun meaning "climate." *Whether* is a conjunction meaning "if." Examples: We don't know *whether* or not they plan to attend; it depends on the *weather.*

where, were. *Where* is an adverb or conjunction involving place. Example: *Where* do you want to sit? *Were* is the plural past tense form of "to be." Example: We *were* all ready to leave.

who, whom. Use *who* when referring to the actor (subject) or complement. Examples: *Who* called? This is *who?* Use *whom* when referring to the object (receiver of the action). Example: To *whom* do you wish to speak? If in doubt, replace *whom* with *him* to see whether that sounds right.

who, which, that. These are all relative pronouns. *Who* refers to people, and *which* refers to things. Current usage allows using *that* to refer to people or things. Examples: The receptionist *who* answers the phone has a pleasant voice. The product, *which* is new, is selling fast. The group *that* gathered was really upset.

who's, whose. *Who's* is a contraction meaning "who is." Example: *Who's* coming to the meeting? *Whose* is the possessive pronoun. Example: *Whose* turn is it to return the calls?

your, you're. *Your* is the possessive pronoun. Example: *Your* order is ready. *You're* is a contraction meaning *you are.* Example: *You're* at the top of the list.

Careless spelling or inaccurate word choices force readers to translate your meaning. By eliminating this irritation, you also avoid embarrassing errors. *Always* run a spell-check. Then proofread.

Workplace Application

It is a good idea to track words that cause you problems. Put a check in the margin each time you look up a word. Then spend time "reprogramming" your spelling of the word until you no longer have trouble with it.

AVOID THE NEW SPEAK OF CYBERSPACE.

Emoticons—using icons to express emotion in online text—are not appropriate in workplace writing. Although some, such as the smiley face ☺, are familiar, most are not. Most readers would not recognize the following: :-@ (angry), :-Z (sleeping), or =:-I (punk rocker). The same is true of online chat short-hand: BTW ("by the way") may be common, but DIY ("do it yourself") and AFAYK ("as far as you know") are not. Reader-friendly writers avoid creating translation problems.

Editing

Word Form

Correct the following sentences for spelling errors and problems of word choice.

1. Part of the chorus went, "How bazaar, how bazaar."

_____

_____

2. He also informed me the "Roscoe" was miss-spelled.

_____

_____

3. If you have any questions in the mean time, please give me a call at 555-4576.

_____

_____

4. The moving of this bed is scaring the walls and the wood doors in the station.

_____

_____

5. For the most part, folk culture depicts rural people in extremely tight-nit family with strong clan ties.

_____

_____

ELEMENTS OF EXCELLENCE

Chapter 5 focused on how you can edit your writing to make it more concise and appropriate. This chapter explained the following points:

> Editing is vital to your success as a proficient professional writer. Polishing your writing ensures that your readers will understand.

> There are appropriate and inappropriate writing styles in professional writing; minimize jargon, use plain language, and keep your "voice" positive.

> Writing is an art—and part of that art is knowing how to prune judiciously.

> The English language can be tricky. A key to successful writing is checking for word demons—the common errors that are preventable. ■

I think the following rules will cover most cases:

1. Never use a metaphor, simile, or other figure of speech which you are used to seeing in print.
2. Never use a long word where a short one will do.
3. If it is possible to cut a word out, always cut it out.
4. Never use the passive where you can use the active.
5. Never use a foreign word, a scientific word, or a jargon word if you can think of an everyday English equivalent.
6. Break any of these rules sooner than say anything outright barbarous.

GEORGE ORWELL
"POLITICS AND THE ENGLISH
LANGUAGE," 1945

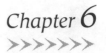
Refining

Potential Problems	Strategies
Incorrect and unfocused sentence structure	➤ Write complete sentences. ➤ Use clear modifiers. ➤ Put main idea in sentence core.
Rambling sentences	➤ Limit most sentences to one main idea, with modifiers. ➤ Do not let sentences run on.
Uninteresting sentences	➤ Vary sentence length. ➤ Carefully place details. ➤ Use parallel structure for series or sentence balance.
Distracting sentence errors	➤ Proofread carefully for grammatical correctness, punctuation, and spelling.

Refining

Refining

Refining

Refining Sentences

What do you notice most? Good writing or poor writing? Most people answer, "Poor—because it is distracting." The irony is that if you write well, readers may not notice. They will be focusing on what you said, not how you said it.

The final step in the writing process involves refining your document to make sure that your readers are not distracted by errors. This chapter presents what you need to know about removing the impurities from your written product. It outlines the most common errors in sentence structure, word formation, punctuation, and mechanics. For answers to more complex or unusual questions about grammar and mechanics, you should consult a good reference manual.

> By the work one
> knows the workman.
>
> JEAN DE LA FORTAINE

At this Refining—or quality control—stage of the writing process, you should revise your written product for clarity and correctness in the following areas.

Sentence Structure

> Fragments
> Comma splices or fused sentences
> Run-on sentences
> Dangling modifiers
> Parallel structure

Word Formation

> Verb forms
> Subject-verb agreement
> Pronoun usage
> Spelling

Punctuation

> End punctuation
> Commas
> Colons
> Semicolons
> Apostrophes
> Hyphens
> Quotation marks

Mechanics

> Numbers
> Dates
> Abbreviations
> Capitalization

Self-Assessment: Grammar and Punctuation

Many people worry about the effectiveness of their grammar. To determine how well you catch errors, correct the following memo. After you feel that you have found all of the grammatical errors, compare your changes to the corrected version at the end of the chapter.

> Many factors influence the distinction between reading that is easy and reading that is hard. Unfamiliar words will cause a stumble. The sentence that is needlessly long will steal our attention. Strange foreign phrases, obscure allusions, inapt quotations, patent errors in grammar or spelling—all these are enemies to pleasant comprehension.
>
> JAMES J. KILPATRICK

Judy Smith and myself was discussing the suspension of employees when they take an in service withdrawal of the Investment Plus or Thrift Plan. Judy would like to know what procedures for the group is in place for Tom Johnson and/or the payroll department, etc. to start and stop a suspension.

I recently sent a memo to Susan Thompson regarding a employee currently suspended in the thrift plan so that their suspension would not be interrupt do to the changes in the Plan, I've attached a copy of the memo sent to Susan for you information.

Also do we continue to in put the "Thrift Plan Date" on Benefit's screen 3 when employee initially joins the plan. And if we are to continue. How do we know when an employee joins the Plan so we can input this date in to the program?

Thanks for your help in this matters.

Controlling Sentences

English sentences are constructed following formulas that place words in certain order. As speakers and writers of English, we can use these formulas to control sentence correctness and to write more interesting and effective sentences.

Fragments

Write complete sentences, not fragments. Sentence fragments do not express a complete thought, even though they may include a subject and a verb. Adding an introductory word such as *because, if, since, that,* or *who* makes a clause dependent, or no longer a complete thought. In other fragments, the verb phrase is incomplete.

Independent Clause: He sent me the report.

Dependent Clauses: *Because* he sent me the report.
If he sent me the report.
Although he sent me the report.

Subordinating conjunctions such as *because, when, if,* and *although* create adverbial dependent clauses.

. . . *that* he sent me the report.
. . . *who* sent me the report.

Relative pronouns such as *that, who,* and *which* create adjective dependent clauses.

Verb Phrases: The manager *having sent* me the report.
The manager *to complete* the report.

Verbal phrases (participles and infinitives) act as modifiers and cannot stand alone.

To correct sentence fragments, connect the incomplete phrase or clause to a complete clause. Or change the word or phrase so that the sentence can stand alone:

Fragment: *Because* he sent me the report.
Correct: *Because* he sent me the report, I could finish the project.

Fragment: The manager *having sent* me the report.
Correct: The manager *had sent* me the report.

Refining

Comma Splices and Fused Sentences

Correct the punctuation in comma splices and fused sentences. In sentences that have two or more independent clauses, you can punctuate the independent clauses in three ways. The last two form compound sentences.

1. With a period to form separate sentences:
   He sent me a report. However, it was incomplete.

2. With a comma and coordinating conjunction:
   [*and, or, but, so, yet, for*]
   He sent me a report, but it was incomplete.

3. With a semicolon:
   [Transitional words such as *therefore* and *then* can be used with this option, but are not required.]
   He sent me a report; however, it was incomplete.

Using a comma or no punctuation between full sentences creates errors called the comma splice or fused sentence.

Comma Splice: He sent me a report, however, it was incomplete.

Fused Sentence: He sent me a report however, it was incomplete.

Correct: He sent me a report. However, it was incomplete.
He sent me a report; however, it was incomplete.

These sentence errors confuse readers because they do not clearly separate equally important ideas.

Do not confuse the semicolon with the colon. These punctuation marks show very different relationships within the sentence.

> The semicolon, like the fulcrum on a seesaw, balances two complete sentences with *equal, closely related* ideas.

> *We have undergone some major changes in our area; therefore, I need to monitor this desk more closely during the transition.*

Rules of the Sentence Punctuation Road

- A period is a stop sign.
- A comma is a yield sign.
- A semicolon is a rolling stop—legal in grammar!

> The colon, like a dam, separates an abstract concept in a complete sentence from the specific details that explain it. It reveals an *unequal* relationship.

We have undergone some major changes in our area: reducing staff, adjusting responsibilities, and eliminating all travel and entertainment expenses.

Sentence Errors

Purpose: This exercise checks your ability to correct sentence errors. Correct the following sentences.

1. They shipped more than we ordered, I don't know why they would issue a credit.

Solution: They shipped more than we ordered. I don't know why they would issue a credit.

2. I hope to receive your answer next week if not I'll call you then we can discuss the project.

Solution: I hope to receive your answer next week. If not, I'll call you so we can discuss the project.

3. I would like two sets of pictures of your establishment. One for my files and one to send in to an architectural magazine.

Solution: I would like two sets of pictures of your establishment: one for my files and one to send in to an architectural magazine. ■

Focus your meaning on the core sentence elements—the subject and verb—to avoid awkward sentences. The simplest sentences have only a subject and verb plus possibly an object or complement.

She ran.
George bought a car.
He is a good worker.

This primer style is correct but boring. As we mature as writers, we learn to add modifiers to sentences, thus adding details and more interesting rhythms.

She ran away from the very large, teeth-baring dog.
Because he could not stand another long walk to work, George bought a car.
In spite of rumors that he landed the job with his family connections, he handles all tasks well except typing.

Identifying the subject and verb is helpful not because you need to know grammatical terms to write sentences. You do not. But it does help you focus awkward sentences. Often you can untangle a sentence by finding the subject and verb, then asking, "Is that my central idea?" You may also ask, "Is that a complete sentence?" If not, think about what you *are* trying to say. Then focus your point in the sentence core.

Vary your sentence structure. Recognizing the core elements also helps you add variety to your sentences. If every sentence begins with a subject-verb construction, the effect is boring. Just as sentences should vary in length, so too they should avoid a repetitious structure. Notice that in this and the previous section, the sentences vary in length, in complexity, in opening elements, in core elements, and in use of parallel structure.

A good rule of thumb is that sentences should average no more than 21 words. That means you will have long sentences, but they will be offset by short ones. Put really important points in short sentences—for emphasis.

Combine short, choppy sentences. To avoid sentences that sound like a first-grade primer, combine ideas to modify one main point. The exception is if you have two or more equally important ideas you want to balance. Then you would use a compound sentence.

Primer Style: *Mark the check void. Then put a note on the check as to the reason that we have voided the check out. (It was a duplicate payment.) Send the check to Tom Smith, 154 S. Main, mc e111, Center City, OK 74103. Or send it to me. It will be backed off the account.*

Revised: *Mark the check void, and then put a note on the check about why we have voided it out (duplicate payment). Send the check to Tom Smith, 154 S. Main, mc e111,*

Center City, OK 74103 or to me. It will be backed off
the account.

Break up run-on sentences. Run-on, or overcombined, sentences present too many ideas for the reader to remember. These ideas need to be divided into shorter sentences for reader clarity.

Run-on: *The operator I spoke with was Shirley and after giving*
her all the background information she told me it would
be perfectly okay to do this and would make all the
necessary changes on the computer.

Revised: *I spoke with the operator Shirley. After I explained all*
the background information, she said doing this would
be perfectly okay. She would make all the necessary
changes in the computer.

Sentence Focus

Purpose: This exercise checks your ability to clarify and focus sentence structure. Revise these sentences to focus ideas more clearly.

1. According to our station attendant on duty at the time of the accident, Mr. Jones saw a girl that he knew and sped away from the pumps in great haste in order to catch up with her and was certainly not paying attention to safe driving when he collided with the very obvious utility pole.

Solution: According to our station attendant on duty at the time of the accident, Mr. Jones saw a girl that he knew and sped away from the pumps in great haste to catch up with her. He was certainly not paying attention to safe driving when he collided with the very obvious utility pole.

2. Our board room has an SL-1 phone and should not be unplugged.

Solution: Our board room has an SL-1 phone, which should not be unplugged.

3. If so, are the calculations the same, and in addition to the reports enclosed, what additional reports are necessary to assist management in controlling inventories?

Solution: If so, are the calculations the same? In addition to the enclosed reports, what additional reports are necessary to assist management in controlling inventories? ∎

Dangling and Misplaced Modifiers

Connect dangling and misplaced modifiers to the words they modify. Recognizing dangling or misplaced modifiers can be tricky. A descriptive modifier must connect to the word it modifies. If the word is implied or buried elsewhere in the sentence, the modifier will dangle, possibly confusing or amusing the reader. Example: *Having rotted in the basement, my brother carried the potatoes to the kitchen.*

Dangling: *Therefore, I respectfully request that you forward me at your earliest convenience the materials for that course. If not available, a refund of the $150 is appreciated.*
[Was the refund not available?]

Correct: *Therefore, please send me the materials for the course at your earliest convenience. If they are not available, please refund the $150.*

Dangling: *By closing our books at the end of the calendar year, our tax accounting was simplified.* [Who closed the books?]

Correct: *Because we closed our books at the end of the calendar year, our tax accounting was simplified.*

Correct: *Closing our books at the end of the year simplified our tax accounting.*

Misplaced: *The employee was wiping off the end of a pipe that had fallen into the mud with his gloved hand.*
[Is his hand lying in the mud?]

Correct: *With his gloved hand, the employee was wiping off the end of a pipe that had fallen into the mud.*

Dangling Modifiers

Purpose: Revise these sentences so that the modifiers are connected clearly to the words they modify and the sentences are punctuated correctly.

1. Central Technology's Year End is June 30, 200__, ALL CLASSES prior to this date must be turned in before June 29, 200__, to be eligible for assistance.

Solution: Central Technology's Year End is June 30, 200__. To be eligible for assistance, you must turn in all earlier classes before June 29, 200__.

2. Hoping to improve the group's safety record, the training sessions were scheduled for five consecutive weeks.

Solution: Hoping to improve the group's safety record, we scheduled the training sessions for five consecutive weeks.

3. Recently, the Sales Representative for my accounts promised my client that the operations team could and would perform a manual process without receiving approval from the Operations Manager.

Solution: Recently, without receiving approval from the operations manager, the sales representatives for my accounts promised my client the operations team could and would perform a manual process. ▪

Parallel Structure

Create parallel structure for items in a series or in balance. Parallel structure occurs when several words, phrases, or clauses are deliberately arranged in a similar structure to support similar content. Strong parallel structure creates clarity and emphasis.

Refining

> The new debenture provided cash *to expand the current assets* and *to retire short-term debt.*
> [*repeated verbal phrases*]

> Typically the drugs are ones that the larger pharmaceutical companies do not want to make *because the market is too small, the delivery media is uncommon, or some other complicating matter makes them unattractive.*
> [*series of dependent clauses*]

> Data Systems and Processing will:

1. *Perform* a technical review and, if required, *ensure* that the proposed hardware and/or software is compatible with existing systems.

2. *Review* the required economic justification.

3. *Work* with the appropriate corporate department to obtain the required approvals.
   [*series based on action verbs*]

Parallelism creates correctness and readability problems if:

> A series presents similar ideas in different structures:

Faulty: Implementing vendor-specific validations will:
   a. *Decrease* error/rejection rates.
   b. *Necessitating* fewer supplements and less provisioning/ vendor communications.
   c. *Decrease* both order cost and order time.
   d. *This will allow us* greater applicability of our forms since our agreements are only valid for clean (error-free) orders.

Correct: Implementing vendor-specific validations will:
   a. *Decrease* error/rejection rates.
   b. *Necessitate* fewer supplements and less provisioning/vendor communication.
   c. *Decrease* both order cost and order time.
   d. *Create* greater applicability of our forms since our agreements are only valid for clean (error-free) orders.

➤ Items in a balanced construction do not match.

Faulty: You have helped thousands of people *not only enjoy their experience* at the zoo, *but also have influenced* how they view wild animals and their relationship to man.

Correct: You *not only have helped thousands* of people enjoy their experience at the zoo, *but also have influenced* how they view wild animals and their relationship to man. [*compound verbs telling what "you" have done*]

YOUR TURN

Sentence Errors

Purpose: The following exercise lets you practice correcting common sentence errors. Correct the following sentences for run-on sentences, fragments, comma splices/fused sentences, dangling modifiers, and parallel structure.

1. I will retain copies of your requests and should these people desire to schedule a class in January, I will place them at the top of the list.

Solution: I will retain copies of your requests. Should these people desire to schedule a class in January, I will place them at the top of the list.

2. Our concerns are many, but heading the list is possible equipment damage and if something does happen to our #3 pump it is conceivable that we simply would not be able to bring on another pump, unless we could convince the electric company to crank up the voltage.

Solution: Our concerns are many, but heading the list is possible equipment damage. If something does happen to our #3 pump, it is conceivable that we simply would not be able to bring on another pump unless we could convince the electric company to crank up the voltage.

3. Hoping this will handle the problem.

Solution: I hope this option will handle the problem.

4. This is a rush, the report is due soon.

Solution: This is a rush because the report is due soon.

5. In an effort to track the number of training hours the staff receives, I would appreciate a quarterly report from you listing employee name, course, and/or seminar completed. Also the number of training hours for your direct reports.

Solution: To track the number of hours the staff receives, I would appreciate a quarterly report from you listing employee name, course and/or seminar completed, and the number of training hours for your direct reports. ■

Controlling Word Forms

Grammar errors are often mistakes in word formation. For example, a missing –s can create a subject-verb agreement error. A dropped –ed makes a verb present tense when it should be past tense. Some errors result from the nonstandard word forms we heard when we were learning to speak. These dialect errors hurt our credibility. This section addresses the common errors that make us look careless and unprofessional.

> Beware the grammar checker on your computer! It can mislead you into thinking something is wrong (like a passive verb or a comma before every "which"). It can also miss errors (such as "it's" vs. "its").
>
> The grammar and spelling checkers are only aids—not substitutes for proofreading.

Using Verbs Correctly

Native speakers of a language are usually unaware of all the rules of verb formation because they acquired the formulas as children. If you do have problems with verbs, remember these tips for consistent and correct usage:

Maintain the same tense in a narrative. Going from past to present to past is distracting for readers.

Incorrect: *Mr. Johnson explained he had been involved in a vehicle accident and the other driver had left the scene of the accident. Mr. Johnson goes on to explain he followed the*

other driver to a location and was now located in front of a
house but is not sure where he was.

Correct: *Mr. Johnson explained he had been involved in a vehicle*
accident and the other driver had left the scene of the
accident. Mr. Johnson went on to explain he followed the
other driver to a location, was now located in front of a
house, but he was not sure where. [*all past tense*]

Choose the simplest form of the verb if you are not implying a special meaning. Simple past can often replace a perfect form.

We went to town instead of *We had gone to town.*

Use auxiliaries such as *must, should,* or *could* to replace wordy phrases.

For example, *We must go* can replace *It is imperative that we go.*

Use the standard forms of verbs to avoid dialect errors.

Incorrect: *We was intending to complete the project this week.*

Correct: *We were intending to complete the project this week.*
[*plural subject and verb*]

Incorrect: *The officer begun to speak.*

Correct: *The officer began to speak.* [*past tense*]

Correct: *The officer had begun to speak.* [*have + the past participle*]

Regular Verbs

Regular verbs follow consistent formation patterns, using the same endings for the different forms of the verb:

Form	Ending	Example
present tense	none = base form	look
3rd person singular, present tense	+ -s	looks
present participle	+ -ing	looking
past tense	+ -ed	looked
past participle	+ -ed	looked

Irregular Verbs

Irregular verbs take many forms. The simple past tense and the past participle, instead of both ending in *-ed,* are different. Also, while the *-en* ending is common in the past participle, it is not universal. To avoid embarrassing dialect errors, you must memorize the correct forms.

Wrong: *We seen him at the cafeteria.*

Right: *We saw him at the cafeteria. [simple past tense]*

We had seen him at the cafeteria every day this week.
[past perfect tense]

Wrong: *The program had ran overnight.*

Right: *The program ran overnight. [simple past tense]*

The program had run overnight. [past perfect tense]

Dictionaries show only the base form for regular verbs but all forms for irregular verbs. Table 6-1 outlines the different forms for common irregular verbs.

TABLE 6-1.   Irregular Verb Forms

Base Form	Present Tense (3rd sing.)	Past Tense	Past Participle	Present Participle
be	am, is, are	was, were	been	being
become	-s	became	become	becoming
begin	-s	began	begun	beginning
blow	-s	blew	blown	blowing
break	-s	broke	broken	breaking
bring	-s	brought	brought	bringing
build	-s	built	built	building
buy	-s	bought	bought	buying
catch	catches	caught	caught	catching
choose	chooses	chose	chosen	choosing
come	-s	came	come	coming
cost	-s	cost	cost	costing
do	does	did	done	doing
drag	-s	dragged	dragged	dragging
draw	-s	drew	drawn	drawing
drink	-s	drank	drunk	drinking
drive	-s	drove	driven	driving
eat	-s	ate	eaten	eating
fall	-s	fell	fallen	falling

(continued)

TABLE 6-1. *(continued)*

Base Form	Present Tense (3rd sing.)	Past Tense	Past Participle	Present Participle
feel	-s	felt	felt	feeling
find	-s	found	found	finding
fly	flies	flew	flown	flying
forget	-s	forgot	forgotten, forgot	forgetting
get	-s	got	gotten, got	getting
give	-s	gave	given	giving
go	goes	went	gone	going
grow	-s	grew	grown	growing
have	has	had	had	having
hear	-s	heard	heard	hearing
hide	-s	hid	hidden	hiding
hit	-s	hit	hit	hitting
hold	-s	held	held	holding
keep	-s	kept	kept	keeping
know	-s	knew	known	knowing
lay ["*to place*" *transitive*]	-s	laid	laid	laying
lead	-s	led	led	leading
lie ["*recline*" *intransitive*]	-s	lay	lain	lying
lose	-s	lost	lost	losing
make	-s	made	made	making
pay	-s	paid	paid	paying
prove	-s	proved	proven	proving
read [rēd]	-s	read [rĕd]	read [rĕd]	reading
ride	-s	rode	ridden	riding
rise	-s	rose	risen	rising
run	-s	ran	run	running
say	-s	said	said	saying
see	-s	saw	seen	seeing
sell	-s	sold	sold	selling
send	-s	sent	sent	sending
set ["*place*" *transitive*]	-s	set	set	setting
sing	-s	sang	sung	singing
sit [*intransitive*]	-s	sat	sat	sitting
sleep	-s	slept	slept	sleeping
speak	-s	spoke	spoken	speaking
stand	-s	stood	stood	standing
strike	-s	struck	struck, stricken	striking
swear	-s	swore	sworn	swearing
take	-s	took	taken	taking
teach	teaches	taught	taught	teaching
tell	-s	told	told	telling
think	-s	thought	thought	thinking

Refining

Base Form	Present Tense (3rd sing.)	Past Tense	Past Participle	Present Participle
throw	-s	threw	thrown	throwing
understand	-s	understood	understood	understanding
wear	-s	wore	worn	wearing
write	-s	wrote	written	writing

TABLE 6-1. *(continued)*

Active versus Passive Voice

Prefer active to passive verbs. Even though grammar checkers highlight passive verbs—as if they are wrong—they are perfectly correct grammatically. However, using too many passive verbs adds unnecessary words and robs your sentences of the energy derived from "Who or what does what to whom" (active voice). Refer to Chapter 5 for practice in transforming passive voice to active voice.

With verbs in the passive voice, the subject (S) of the sentence receives the action of the verb (V), and the actor is in an actual or implied "by" prepositional phrase (see Table 6-2).

> Good grammar, I suggest, equates with good manners. Try not to belch at the table, darling, and do remember that a singular subject demands a singular verb. For good or ill, we are betrayed by our speech.
>
> JAMES J. KILPATRICK

TABLE 6-2. Passive Voice versus Active Voice

Subject	Passive Voice S-V		Active Voice S-V-O
	Form of *to be* as the auxiliary	Main verb in past participle form	
Susan	*is (present tense)*	*admired by all.*	*All admire Susan.*
The report	*was (past tense)*	*written in Spanish.*	*He wrote the report in Spanish.*
The test	*will be (future tense)*	*given today.*	*I will give the test today.*

Refining

Subject-Verb Agreement

In English, the subject (S) of a sentence must agree with the verb (V) in number. If the subject is plural, the verb must be too. This rule seems easy enough to observe, but other structures in English complicate the issue.

> Plural nouns end in *s,* but singular verbs in the present tense also end in *s.* This apparent contradiction can be confusing.

> The *girls* love ice cream.
>
> The girl *loves* ice cream.

> The subject and verb are often separated by words or clauses that explain the subject:

Subject   [+ modifiers]   + Verb
The accountant [in the front office] called.

Sometimes nouns closer to the verb seem to be the subject. It is easy to make the verb agree with the nearest noun instead of the real subject.

Incorrect: The *list* of reports *are enclosed.*

Correct: The *list* of reports *is enclosed.*

> By definition, some pronouns are singular (*each, everyone, everybody*), whereas others are plural (*all, both, some*). *None* can be singular or plural, depending on the context.

Each of them *is planning* to play a part.

All of them *are planning* to play a part.

None of the shipment *is* in the warehouse.

None of us *are planning* to attend.

Everyone is planning to go.

> Sometimes the subject and verb are reversed. Because the first word (in the normal subject slot) does not end in *s,* it is easy to assume that the verb should be singular.

There *are* several *suggestions* to consider.
     V   S

Enclosed are the *reports* you requested.
  V   S

Attached is the *invoice* you are expecting.
  V   S

> Compound subjects with *and* always take a plural verb. If neither subject ends in *s,* it is easy to assume the verb should be singular.

The *report* on our status and the *list are* correct.
   S   S V

> For compound subjects with *or* or *nor,* the verb agrees with the subject closest to it.

          S   S   V
Either the *report* on our status or the *lists* of attendees *are* incorrect.

         S   S   V
Neither the *lists* of attendees nor the *report* on our status *is* correct.

> Subjects consisting of phrases or dependent clauses always take singular verbs.

Running a large company is a complex task.
            S   V

How we will build a consensus is the main agenda item.
            S   V

> The verb in a dependent adjective clause agrees with the noun that *who, whom, which,* or *that* refers to.

     S   *adjective clause*   V
The *woman who is training our staff likes* to have music playing in the room.

Some examples:

Incorrect: Once again, your *time and consideration is* appreciated.

Correct: Once again, your *time and consideration are* appreciated.

Incorrect:	The process halts when *one* of a set of user-defined conditions *are met.*
Correct:	The process halts when *one* of a set of user-defined conditions *is met.*
Incorrect:	The *manner* in which the loans are processed *are* as follows.
Correct:	The *manner* in which the loans are processed *is* as follows.
Correct:	The *loans are* processed as follows.
Incorrect:	There *is* no available *employees* that can perform these tasks.
Correct:	There *are* no available *employees* that can perform these tasks.
Correct:	No *employees are* available who can perform these tasks.

YOUR TURN

Subject-Verb Agreement

Purpose: The following exercise asks you to correct subject-verb errors. Correct the subject-verb agreement errors in the following sentences:

1. On July 2, 200__, a notification letter requesting receipts for this month were sent to you.

Solution: On July 2, 200__, a notification letter requesting receipts for this month was sent to you.

2. As sonar technology and laser technology is implemented, additional OT or IT positions will have to be reclassified.

Solution: As sonar technology and laser technology are implemented, additional OT or IT positions will have to be reclassified.

3. Completing the forms do not obligate you to become a volunteer.

Solution: Completing the forms does not obligate you to become a volunteer.

Refining

Pronouns

By definition, a *pronoun* takes the place of a noun. Therefore, to clearly connect ideas, a pronoun follows a noun, clearly refers to it, and agrees with the noun in number.

Make a pronoun agree in number with the noun it replaces. Noun-pronoun agreement makes our sentences "add up."

Incorrect: Send the *employee* form to *their* attention.

Correct: Send the *employees'* forms to *their* attention.

Correct: Send the form to the employee.

PITFALLS

Should I use *he* or *she, him* or *her,* or should I just say *them?*

Sometimes it is hard to know how to refer to large groups. Whenever possible, avoid referring to readers as all men or women. Alternating from *he* to *she* has become common, although that can seem contrived. The easiest solution is to use the plural *they* and *them.* Even companies have been called *them* for quite a while.

People disagree about how to handle generic, singular nouns such as *employee.* Using the masculine *he* or *him* to refer to all humans is out of date. But so far there is no agreement about an acceptable alternative, such as *they* or the clumsy *he/she.* Your best choices are to make both the noun or pronoun plural if you can, or avoid the issue by using *a* or *the*—for example, "Send the employee a form." ■

Use singular pronouns to refer to collective nouns, such as *group* or *committee* unless a plural meaning is implied.

Incorrect: The *committee* is planning to sponsor *their* golf outing.

Correct: The *committee* is planning to sponsor *its* golf outing.

The *committee* is planning to sponsor *a* golf outing.

The *committee* all stood to accept *their* plaques.

Refining

Use the correct number to refer to indefinite pronouns that are singular (*each, everyone, everybody*) or plural (*all, both, some*). Or avoid using a pronoun.

> *Each* of them is planning to play *his* or *her* part.
>
> *All* of them are planning to play *their* parts.
>
> *All* of them are planning to play *a* part.
>
> *Everyone* is going to wear *his or her* coat.
>
> *Everyone* is going to wear *a* coat.

Make demonstrative pronouns *(this, that, these,* and *those)* clearly refer to a noun and agree with the noun in number.

Incorrect:	The agent offered several *policy options. This* constituted his portfolio.
Correct:	The agent offered several *policy options. These* constituted his portfolio.

Check for pronouns that do not clearly refer to nouns. The pronouns *this, which,* and *it* are often used carelessly to refer to the entire preceding idea rather than to a particular noun. You can easily correct this broad reference and improve clarity by inserting a noun after *this* or before *which.* Replace *it* with a noun.

Vague:	We will begin the project by meeting next week. *This* will enable us to address important questions promptly.
More Clear:	We will begin the project by meeting next week. *This schedule* will enable us to address important questions promptly.
Vague:	The meeting lasted until 6:00 p.m., *which* made me late for dinner.
More Clear:	The meeting lasted until 6:00 p.m., *a delay which* made me late for dinner.
Vague:	To get *it* off the ground, we need to assign responsibilities.
More Clear:	To get *the project* off the ground, we need to assign responsibilities.

Refining

Use personal pronouns in the correct case, or form. The case is determined by the pronoun's function in the sentence, as shown in Table 6-3.

Incorrect: May I speak to Joan? This is *her*.

Correct: May I speak to Joan? This is *she*. [complement]

Correct: If you plan to attend, give *me* a call. [indirect object]

Correct: If you plan to attend, send the card to *me*.
                  [object of the preposition]

TABLE 6-3.   **Cases of Personal and Relative Pronouns**

	Personal Pronouns		
Person	As Subjects and Complements	As Objects	As Possessives
Singular			
1	I	me	my, mine
2	you	you	your, yours
3	he	him	his
	she	her	her, hers
	it	it	its
Plural			
1	we	us	our, ours
2	you	you	your, yours
3	they	them	their, theirs
	Relative Pronouns		
	who	whom	whose
	whoever	whomever	whosever
	Note:	Notice that *-m* ends several objective pronouns—*him* is like *whom*.	Notice that *-s* ends several possessive pronouns. No possessive pronoun has an apostrophe, even *its*.

Incorrect:	He had more influence than *me*.
Correct:	He had more influence than *I* [had]. [subject]
Incorrect:	*Him and me* are planning to win the tournament.
Correct:	*He and I* are planning to win the tournament. [subjects]

Who and *whom* have the same cases as *he* and *him*. Try substituting those words as the answer to the question to see what sounds right.

> To whom do you wish to speak? I want to speak to him.
> Who called? *He* called.

Use *who* and *whom* to refer to *people* and *which* to refer to things. *That* may refer to both people and things.

Use the correct case in compound constructions, and put yourself last. To check, drop one part of the compound. If the remaining pronoun does not sound right alone, it probably is not.

Incorrect:	He sent the report to Tom and *I*.
	He sent the report to I?
	He sent the report to Tom and *myself*.
	He sent the report to myself?
	He sent the report to *me* and Tom.
Correct:	He sent the report to Tom and *me*.

Use the possessive pronoun form with gerunds (verbs ending in *-ing* and functioning like a noun).

| **Incorrect:** | The committee members resented *him* talking to the press without their approval. |
| **Correct:** | The committee members resented *his* talking to the press without their approval. |

Use the -*self* pronouns only if there is a doubling in the sentence. These pronouns are correct only when the doer and the receiver refer to the same person or thing (**reflexive**) or when the person's involvement is emphasized (**intensive**).

Reflexive: George gave *himself* a raise.

Intensive: Susan completed the report all by *herself.*

Many people, trying to avoid the *he/him* or *I/me* issue, incorrectly choose a -*self* pronoun:

Wrong: Send the bill to Janet or *myself.*
Right: Send the bill to Janet or *me.*

Wrong: I signed *me* up for the course.
Right: I signed *myself* up for the course.

Wrong: *Myself and Gary* were up for a raise.
Right: *Gary and I* were up for a raise.

Spell-Checking

Everyone has occasional problems with spelling. Often errors come from carelessness, from not taking the time to review what has been written. Some people do not see that the letters have been reversed or omitted. Other spelling errors result from laziness, from not looking up questionable spelling in a dictionary and then memorizing the correct form. In every case, lack of proofreading is the major cause.

Spelling errors would be forgivable if they did not immediately create such a bad impression. Even the best memo—or e-mail—appears inaccurate or illiterate if it is sprinkled with misspelled words. It shouts to the reader, "My writer did not bother with quality control."

Some general suggestions and specific spelling rules may help you avoid creating such a negative impression.

Learn to spell the words you use regularly. Do not allow bad habits to develop in spelling the special vocabulary of your profession or commonly used words.

Buy and use a small dictionary or administrative assistant's spelling guide. When you check on a word's spelling, mark the word in the guide to remind yourself that you needed help. When a word collects several marks, memorize it.

Technology and Effective Spelling

There are a number of word processing software packages that offer their own version of spell-check. While spell-checkers can help you to catch blatantly misspelled words, they miss similarly spelled words (*two, to, too*) as well as diction mistakes (e.g., all intensive purposes versus all intents and purposes).

Be aware that just because your memo or report is "spell-checked," it may not be error-free. ■

Remember some basic word formation rules.

> Plural nouns and acronyms usually end in -*s*. (girl*s*, SST*s*)
> When a noun ends in -*s, -x, -ch, -sh,* or -*z*, add -*es* to form the plural. (wish*es*, church*es*)
> To form a plural when a noun ends in a consonant + -*y*, change the -*y* to -*i* and add -*es. (*copy, cop*ies)*
> Singular nouns that show possession end in -'*s*. (girl'*s*, woman'*s*)
> For plural possessive nouns, form the plural first and then add an apostrophe or -'*s*. (girls', women'*s*)
> Verbs in the past tense often end in -*ed*. (ask*ed*)
> *Double the final consonant* when adding a suffix starting with a vowel to a word ending in a single vowel + a single consonant. (hit/hit*ting*, swim/swim*mer*)
> Words ending in silent -*e* usually drop the -*e* before a suffix beginning with a vowel. (arriv*e*/arriv*al*, argu*e*/argu*ing*)

Always run a spell-check and then proofread carefully. Do not skim over words without seeing them. Read them out loud. Read backward, one word at a time. In other words, be concerned about correct spelling.

Word Formation

Purpose: This exercise asks you to practice correcting errors in word formation. Correct the following sentences, paying particular attention to errors in word formation—spelling, verb forms, subject-verb agreement, and pronoun usage:

1. But as the years have gone by, inflation and other factors has raised the cost of living.

Solution: But as the years have gone by, inflation and other factors have raised the cost of living. [subject-verb agreement]

2. Mr. Johnson explained he had been involved in a vehicle accident and the other driver had left the scene of the accident. Mr. Johnson goes on to explain he followed the other driver to a location and was now located in front of a house but is not sure where he was.

Solution: Mr. Johnson explained that he had been involved in a vehicle accident and the other driver had left the scene of the accident. Mr. Johnson went on to explain that he followed the other driver to a location and was then in front of a house. He was not sure where he was. [consistent verb tense]

3. John told you, Carman Simpson, and myself, he had been on our location at the original meeting.

Solution: John told you, Carmon Simpson, and me that he been at our location for the original meeting. [pronoun form, preposition choice]

4. Circles on the tabulation indicates low bids.

Solution: Circles on the tabulation indicate low bids. [subject-verb agreement]

5. Each suspect stated they received payment for passing the counterfeited checks.

Solution: Both suspects stated they received payment for passing the counterfeited checks. [noun-pronoun agreement]

Refining

Proofreading for Word Errors

Correct all errors in the following memo.

To: Jim Smith

From: Larry Johnson

Date: Jan. 3, 200__

Subject: New Vacation Schedule

Because every one in the Department try to take vacations at Christmas time, we are left understaffed at a busy time of the year. This effects the efficiency of the department and makes it impossible to close the books before the end of the year report.

Next year there are a requirement that every employee should request vacation by their seniorty with only 5 allowed to vacation at Christmas. By seperating vacation times we can avoid the understaffing problem and still allows alot of flexibility in scheduling.

Solution:

To: Jim Smith

From: Larry Johnson

Date: Jan. 3, 200__

Subject: New Vacation Schedule

Because everyone in the department tries to take vacations at Christmas, we are left understaffed at a busy time of the year. This understaffing affects the efficiency of the department and makes it impossible to close the books before the end-of-the-year report.

Next year there is a requirement that every employee should request vacation by seniority, with only five people allowed a vacation at Christmas. By separating vacation times, we can avoid the understaffing problem and still allow a lot of flexibility in scheduling.

Refining

Proofreading

Correct all sentence and word formation errors in the following memo.

> Every motor carrier according to the regulators have to establish a Employee Assistance Program (EAP) for their drivers and supervisor to use.
>
> The EAP is suppose to consist of training programs for the supervisory personal and all drivers. It should include the affects and consequences of using illegal drugs and alcohol in regards to personal health, safety, and the work environment. The program also covers changes that indicates abuse and documentation of training given to the supervisory personal and drivers'.
>
> If you now of an employee which needs help, have them call the following hot line number: 800-555-5151.

Figure 6-1 is a quick reference to the grammatical structures that require punctuation. Though it is not an exhaustive model, it does cover almost all the punctuation you will use in your ordinary writing tasks. If a construction is not listed, you probably do not need punctuation, or it is such an odd usage that even experts have to look it up. Use these Quick Tips as your first reference for punctuation questions. Brackets [ ] mean that an element is optional.

PUNCTUATION COUNTS!

An English professor wrote the words "woman without her man is nothing" on the board and told the students to punctuate it correctly.

The men wrote: "Woman, without her man, is nothing."

The women wrote: "Woman! Without her, man is nothing."

Refining

QUICK TIPS ON PUNCTUATION	
BETWEEN FULL SENTENCES	Sentence. Sentence. Sentence, and/or/but sentence. Sentence; [therefore,] sentence.
COLONS	Sentence/General: specifics/list of details.
COMMAS	Sentence, and sentence. Introductory phrase containing a verb or more than five words, sentence. Transition, sentence. Sentence, shifting modifier. adjective, adjective noun item, item[,] and item Sen-, interrupter, -tence. noun, describing clause, noun specifying clause month day, year, month year
APOSTROPHES	singular noun's apostrophe plural nouns' apostrophe It's a contraction.
HYPHENS	adjective-grouping modifier
NUMBERS	one . . . ten, 11 . . . 1 percent $5 million on June 1
CAPITALS	Proper Name common name

Figure 6-1: Quick tips on punctuation

Punctuation

Period [.]

1. Marks the end of a complete sentence other than a question or exclamation.

2. Is not used for initials of an organization (*USAF*, *IBM*).

3. Is used with abbreviations of words or titles (*a.m.*, *p.m.*, *Dr.*, *Mrs.*).

4. Goes inside quotation marks.

Question Mark [?]

1. Marks the end of a question.

   When do you want to go?

2. Does not mark the end of a rhetorical question that is actually making a request.

   Would you mind completing this form for me.

3. Falls inside or outside quotation marks, depending on the meaning of the sentence.

   She asked, "Do you have time to talk?"
   Is there another chapter besides "Beginnings"?

Exclamation Point [!]

1. Marks the end of a statement of surprise or excitement.

   Wow! We had a great quarter.

2. Should be used sparingly. They can be annoying and lose their impact if overused.

3. Falls inside or outside quotation marks, depending on the meaning of the sentence.

   The sales reps shouted "Yes!"
   Despite all our efforts, we were labeled "losers"!

Colon [:]

1. May introduce a list or series unless "such as," "for example," or some other transitional phrase is used. The colon is usually preceded by a complete sentence.

   We expect these results from the strategy: increased customer base, wider market area, and higher profits.

2. Before an open list (using bullets or numbers), it is no longer necessary to complete the sentence, as long as it flows grammatically into the listed items. Punctuate the list based on its complexity: no marks after single words, commas after short phrases, semicolons after more complex phrases, or periods after full sentences.

   From the strategy, we expected to achieve:
   > *Increased customer base,*
   > *Wider market area,*
   > *Higher profits.*

3. Introduces an explanation; almost the equivalent of "namely," "that is." What is on one side of the colon explains or balances what is on the other side.

   You were right: She is an excellent writer.

4. Introduces a quotation in a more formal way than a comma.

   Code 25, Section 4 states: "The defendant . . ."

5. Do *not* insert a colon between parts of the sentence that belong together (subject and verb, verb and complement).

   Incorrect: *Attendees included: Julius, Samuel, and Theresa.*

6. Follows the salutation in a formal letter. In an informal letter, you may use a comma.

   Dear President Simpson:
   Dear Joe,

Semicolon [;]

1. Separates complete sentences when the meaning is closely related. It functions almost as half a comma and half a period.

   If nominated, I will not run; if elected, I will not serve.

2. Precedes a conjunctive adverb (a transitional word such as *also, however, consequently, therefore*) when connecting complete sentences.

   Our profits are up; therefore, we are reinstating travel allowances.

3. Functions as a strong comma to separate a series of phrases that have internal commas.

   The meeting agenda included reports from Susan Johnson, vice president; Travis Jones, director of marketing; and Cynthia Reynolds, plant superintendent.

Comma [,]

1. Precedes a coordinating conjunction (*and, or, but, so, yet, for*) joining complete sentences.

   The traffic light malfunctioned, and the intersection was a free-for-all.

   Do not use a comma before *and* unless it separates complete sentences. For strong contrast, you may use a comma before an *or* or *but* that does not separate complete sentences.

   We expect to receive your application and a letter of recommendation.

   We expected to receive your application, but did not.

2. Separates an introductory clause or phrase with a verb in it from the main sentence.

   To explain her plan, Marilyn used charts and graphs.

   Because the information was complex, Marilyn used charts and graphs in her presentation.

3. Sets off any introductory phrase of five or more words. With fewer than five words, the comma is optional.

   At the end of the very long meeting, we made some quick decisions.

> Commas are "break marks," not "breath marks." Do not insert a comma every time you pause.

Refining

4. Usually follows transitional words or phrases at the beginning of a sentence or surrounds transitions (*In that case, Therefore, i.e.,*) unless they are very short (*Also* or *Then*).

   Nevertheless, the cost spiral continues.

   Then hit "Enter."

   The invoice arrived late, i.e., on the 30th of the month.

5. May separate a dependent clause or modifying phrase at the end of a sentence if there is a noticeable shift in emphasis.

   I have decided to go ahead with the plan, despite my misgivings.

6. Sets off interrupting expressions or explanations.

   Doctors, I think, have insufficient knowledge of acupuncture.

   Mr. Ball, the president for 25 years, was greatly respected.

   We expect, however, to improve our performance.

7. Indicates describing clauses. Describing clauses give more information about the noun, but can be omitted without changing the meaning of the sentence.

   The desk, which is available at several stores, will improve the office appearance. [*Only one desk is being discussed.*]

   Specifying, or essential, clauses are not set off with commas.

   The desk which needs to be moved is in the corner. [*There are at least two desks, but only the one in the corner needs to be moved.*]

   Traditional grammar made a distinction between *which* to introduce describing adjective clauses and *that* to introduce specifying adjective clauses. However, current practice no longer makes that distinction. You must look to the meaning to determine whether a modifier describes or specifies.

8. Sets off direct quotations.

   She said, "Please send me a memo."

   Do not use a comma to set off an indirect quotation.

   She said that I should send her a memo.

9. Separates each item in a series. The comma before the *and* at the end of a series may be omitted if the meaning is clear (journalists' style). [*See "Semicolon" for complex series punctuation.*]

   She bought a dress, a pair of sandals, and a purse to match.

10. Separates simple adjectives describing the same noun.

    She wrote a pretty, good report. [*It was pretty and good.*]

    Not: She wrote a pretty good report. [*Neither pretty nor good*]

11. Sets off *yes, no,* and *etc.*

    No, I will not agree to meet, talk, etc., until next week.

12. Sets off words of direct address.

    Joe, meet me at the corner.

13. Separates two parts of a geographical location and follows names of states or countries.

    She was born in New York, NY, in 1986.

14. Sets off the year from the month and day. Do not use between month and year only.

    Tuesday, June 10, 2003,   but   ***June 2003***

15. No longer follows a year unless the month and day are also stated.

    In 2003 you wrote that . . .   but   ***On July 20, 2003, you wrote . . .***

16. Follows the salutation and complimentary close.

17. Goes inside closing quotation marks.

Dash [—]

1. In typed text, a dash is two hyphens: —

2. Indicates an abrupt break. Use it sparingly. The material within dashes is very emphatic.

   The courtroom—that hallowed hall of justice—is too often backlogged.

3. Can serve like a colon, as a pause before a series. This use is appropriate only in informal or very expressive writing.

Children can make mischief in any place—on the yard, at school, in church.

Parentheses [( )]

1. Deemphasize material. Information in parentheses is less essential than if set off by commas.

The minimum fabric overlap requirement of 2 longitudinal wire spaces = 2" (i.e., 1"–2") will not be met.

2. If the parenthetical information is a full sentence and stands alone, the end punctuation is inside the parentheses. However, if the parentheses end a sentence and complete it, the period or other end mark is outside the final parenthesis.

(See Chapter 5 for a full explanation.)

While in our city (he has since returned to Los Angeles), the film director shot several commercials about our local attractions.

3. Do not use to explain pronouns.

Wrong: *He (Jones) was young.*

Write instead: *Jones was young.*

4. Do not break up a sentence with a long parenthesis because the reader will lose track of the main idea.

Apostrophe [']

1. Indicates noun possession. For a singular noun, add *'s.*

A week's work, an employee's office, IBM's strategy

2. To form the possessive of plural nouns:

If the word ends in *-s,* add only an apostrophe: *the Smiths' house* [*not* The Smith's], *the assistants' desks*

If the plural does not end in *-s,* add an apostrophe and an *-s: women's shoes*

3. For nouns ending in -s, -cks, -x, or -z, say the word out loud and notice if you are adding an -s. If you add -s when you say it, add an apostrophe and -s when you write it:

Jesus' parables, the boss's office

4. Do *not* add an apostrophe to personal pronouns.

his book, its alternative

5. Do use the apostrophe to show indefinite pronouns' possession.

one's hopes, others' opinions

6. Indicates the letters or numbers left out of a contraction.

He didn't do it. The class of '90. It's your move.

7. Do not add an apostrophe for a plural acronym.

We issued three RFPs.

Hyphen [-]

1. Connects adjectives functioning as one-word descriptions and preceding the noun:

out-of-date report, short-term profit, company-owned plane

If the last word is a verb form, the phrase will be hyphenated no matter where it is in the sentence:

The new plane is company-owned.

Exception—If the first word ends in -*ly,* do not use a hyphen:

It was a widely accepted theory.

2. In a series of phrases sharing a common word, suspend the hyphen on the first and then complete the second hyphenated phrase: ***short- and long-term plans.***

3. No longer attaches most prefixes or suffixes: ***cooperate, preretirement, coworker, companywide***.

Attaches prefixes or suffixes in a few instances: ***all-knowing, pro-ERA, self-made***. Check your dictionary, *The Gregg Reference Manual,* or another standard office reference.

4. Is always used after prefixes before a proper name:
   anti-American.

5. Because of computers' word-wrap function, we rarely divide words at the end of a line. However, if you must, remember these guidelines for word division:

   ➤ Divide between syllables.
   ➤ Do not divide a one-syllable word or separate a single letter.

Ellipses [. . .]

1. Indicate words omitted from quoted text.

2. Do not use, even in casual e-mails, to indicate a pause.

Mechanics

Numbers

1. Spell out numbers from *one* to *ten,* and use numerals above *ten:* ***one . . . ten, 11. . . .*** If numbers above and below *ten* occur in the same sentence, be consistent.
   We ordered copies of the 15 notebooks.
   We ordered 6 copies each of the 15 notebooks.

2. Never start a sentence with a numeral. Spell out the number or rearrange the sentence.

3. Percents always use numerals followed by *percent,* unless in a technical calculation where the % symbol is appropriate.

4. Use numerals in writing about money, measurement, dates, fractions, or other technical data.

5. There is no need to repeat numbers in parentheses [e.g., *ten (10)*] unless the document is a contract or specifications.

Dates

1. Use only numerals for the day, without *st, nd, th,* etc., in normal month, day, year order: ***September 1, 200___***

2. Use the *st, nd, th,* etc., if the day precedes the month:
   the 1st of September

Abbreviations

1. Use abbreviations sparingly, especially with words that are normally spelled out:
   ***December*, not Dec.; *government*, not govt.**

2. Most acronyms (letters replacing names) do not use periods:
   IBM, RFP, PC

3. Use periods after the letters in lower case abbreviations:
   a.m., p.m., etc., e.g., i.e.

4. If an abbreviation occurs at the end of the sentence, only one period is needed.

Capitalization

1. Capitalize proper names, i.e., the unique name of a person or entity:
   Bessie Thompson, the Marketing Department, July, Widget Manufacturing

2. Do not capitalize common nouns, i.e., a generic name:
   my mother, our department, this month, our company

3. Job titles are not capitalized, except in formal documents such as minutes of meetings:
   The manager of the Accounting Department called a meeting for 2:00 p.m.

4. Capitalize the form words but not the structure words in titles and subject lines:
   Subject: Budget Report Due in Two Weeks

5. Capitalize the first word of a sentence. Do not capitalize the first word following a colon unless it begins a full sentence.

6. Capitalize the first word in each item in a list, even if it is a single word.

7. Capitalize only the first word of a complimentary closing:
   Thank you, Very truly yours,

8. For state names in addresses, use the U.S. Postal Service abbreviations with two capitals and no periods: *FL, NY, OK, TX*, and so on.

Corrected Self-Assessment *(p. 127)*

Judy Smith and **I** [*pronoun form*] **were** [*subject-verb agreement*] discussing the suspension of employees when they take an in-service [*hyphen*] withdrawal of the Investment Plus or Thrift Plan. Judy would like to know what procedures for the group **are** [*subject-verb agreement*] in place for Tom Johnson or [*unnecessary contrast*] the **P**ayroll **D**epartment [*proper name*], etc., [*comma after etc.*] to start and stop a suspension.

I recently sent a memo to Susan Thompson regarding a**n** [*an before vowel sound*] employee currently suspended in the Thrift Plan [*proper name*] so that **his** [*noun-pronoun agreement*] suspension would not be interrupt**ed** [*verb form*] **due** [*spelling*] to the changes in the **p**lan [common noun]. [*comma splice*] I've attached a copy of the memo sent to Susan for your [*possessive pronoun*] information.

Also, [*comma after transition*] do we continue to **input** [*spelling*] the "Thrift Plan Date" on **the** [*omitted word*] **Benefits Screen 3** [*screen name; not possessive*] when the [*omitted word*] employee initially joins the plan**?** [*question*] If we are to continue, [*fragment*] how do we know when an employee joins the plan [*common noun*] so we can input this date **into** [*spelling*] the program?

Thanks for your help in **these** [*agreement*] matters.

The original had 25 errors. How did you do?

Missed 0 to 2—Great job, grammar guru.
Missed 3 to 5—Pretty sharp eye, but you need to concentrate.
Missed 6 to 8—You're okay but a little rusty. This chapter will help.
Missed 9 or more—Now is your chance to improve those proofreading skills.

ELEMENTS OF EXCELLENCE

Chapter 6 focused on how you can refine your documents. This chapter explained the following quality-control points:

> Sometimes sentence structure is complicated, but you can straighten out ill-conceived sentences.
> Correct grammar is vital to clear communication. People who receive your documents will make assumptions about you as a professional.
> While punctuation may seem basic, appropriately using these marks is important. This chapter updated you on proper punctuation.

Refining

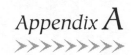

Reader-Friendly Writing Checklist

In **Planning and Organizing**, have you:

- Thought about your readers and purpose?
- Stated your main idea in the first paragraph?
- Arranged your key points logically?
- Mentioned the specific action you want?

Have you **Written** paragraphs that:

- Begin with strong topic sentences?
- Present specific details to explain your key points?
- Stick to one topic?
- Use clear transitions and logical order?
- Employ white space and other design features to emphasize points?

In **Editing**, have you:

- Checked for spelling and precise word choice?
- Watched your jargon and chosen a direct, personal voice?
- Edited for conciseness by choosing strong, action verbs and pruning extra words?

In **Refining**, have you:

- Checked grammatical correctness (fragments, comma splices, subject-verb agreement, pronoun reference)?
- Reviewed spelling, punctuation, and mechanics?
- Set up a format for the final document that will make the reader's job easy?

Proofreader's Marks

Mark	Draft	Final
for Editing		
Delete	The ~~very~~ unique plan	The unique plan
Delete a letter and close up	An unexpected honor	An unexpected honor
Insert	A ^rough draft copy	A rough draft copy
Spell out	The 2-day conference	The two-day conference
Add on to a word	She was real good at hedging.	She was really good at hedging.
Delete a space	It is so obvious	It is so obvious
Insert a space	It is obvious	It is not obvious
Move as shown	It is not true.	It is true.
Let it stand (do not change)	It is not true.	It is not true.
Start a new paragraph	That was the conclusion. However, the next day the plan changed . . .	That was the conclusion. However, the next day the plan changed . . .
for Refining		
Transpose	recieve	receive
Lowercase a letter	. . . for her State taxes.	. . . for her state taxes.
Capitalize a letter	. . . for her texas taxes.	. . . for her Texas taxes.
Insert a period	Ms. Joan Smith	Ms. Joan Smith
Insert a comma	Ms. Smith the chief financial officer attended.	Ms. Smith, the chief financial officer, attended.
Insert an apostrophe	The plans outcome is uncertain.	The plan's outcome is uncertain.
Insert quotation marks	She said, Great.	She said, "Great."
Insert a hyphen	It is a two day conference.	It is a two-day conference.

Proofreader's Marks

Mark	Draft	Final

for Refining (continued)

Mark	Draft	Final
; / Insert semicolon	They expected her to go; however, she did not.	They expected her to go; however, she did not.
: / Insert colon	. . . ran three tests: a, b, and c	. . . ran three tests: a, b, and c.
—ₘ Insert a dash or change a hyphen to a dash	She won—finally.	She won—finally.
( ) Insert parentheses	Send it today (May 30).	Send it today (May 30).

for Formatting

Mark	Draft	Final
ss[Single-space	ss[He said to come. But I refused.	He said to come. But I refused.
DS[Double-space	DS[He said to come. But I refused.	He said to come. But I refused.
∨ Raise above the line	The 21st day	The 21st day
∧ Drop below the line	H₂O	H_2O
ital. Use italics	The Writing Coach *ital.*	*The Writing Coach*
bf Use bold face	I will not.	I will **not**.
⌐ Move to the right	⌐ $434.67	$434.67
⌐ Move to the left	[$434.67	$434.67
2⌐ Indent 2 spaces	George Vicas 2⌐ the guest of honor	George Vicas the guest of honor
)) Align horizontally	Calling all campers!	Calling all campers!
‖ Align vertically	‖ Ellen Schwartz Richard Rodriguez	Ellen Schwartz Richard Rodriguez
]Ε Center	]Menu[	Menu
fl Flush left	fl Your honor:	Your honor:
fr Flush right	fr August 7, 200_	August 7, 200_

Index

The Five O'Clock Club Series

Kate Wendleton

Celebrating 25 years as America's Premier Career Coaching and Outplacement Network for Professionals, Managers and Executives

Not your average job search guides, the Five O'Clock Club books offer advice from professional career coaches, with over 25 years experience advising and placing professionals, executives and career-changers. Kate Wendleton presents proven strategies for maximizing the interview; developing your career within your present organization; getting networking interviews with decision-makers; creating a resume; identifying the right career; and teaching methods for getting the perfect job. Numerous case studies make the content real, and easy to apply to *your* job search.

The Five O'Clock Club books give you the knowledge you need to:

* Develop your own "accomplishment statement" that you can use in your resume, cover letters, interviews, and more
* Create a winning resume that gets you in-person meetings
* Use the internet to effectively research your targets
* Secure informational meetings and networking interviews with organization decision-makers
* Gain power in the interview process
* Turn interviews into offers
* Use Kate's Four-Step Salary Negotiation Method
* Enhance your interpersonal skills to survive and thrive once you get the job

Mastering the Job Interview and Winning the Money Game
ISBN: 1-4180-1500-8

Navigating Your Career: Develop Your Plan, Manage Your Boss, Get Another Job Inside
ISBN: 1-4180-1501-6

Shortcut Your Job Search: The Best Way to Get Meetings
ISBN: 1-4180-1502-4

Packaging Yourself: The Targeted Résumé
ISBN: 1-4180-1503-2

Targeting a Great Career
ISBN: 1-4180-1504-0

Launching the Right Career
ISBN: 1-4180-1505-9

258 pp., 7 3/8" x 9 1/4", softcover

About the Author:

Kate Wendleton is a nationally syndicated careers columnist and recognized authority on career development, having appeared on *The Today Show*, CNN, CNBC, *Larry King Live*, National Public Radio, CBS, and in the *New York Times, Chicago Tribune, Wall Street Journal, Fortune, Business Week,* and other national media. She has been a career coach since 1978 when she founded The Five O' Clock Club and developed its methodology to help job hunters and career changers at all levels. This methodology is now used throughout the US and Canada where Five O' Clock Club members meet regularly. Kate is also the founder of Workforce America, a not-for-profit organization serving adult job hunters in Harlem. A former CFO of two small companies, Kate has twenty years of business experience, as well as an MBA.

www.delmarlearning.com

To place an order please call: (800) 347-7707 or fax: (859) 647-5963
Mailing Address: Thomson Distribution Center, Attn: Order Fulfillment, 10650 Toebben Dr., Independence, KY 41051